Emotional Intelligence

2 Books in 1

The Best Guide on How To Use Emotional Intelligence For a Better Life, Success At Work, Improve Your Social Skill and Cultivating Effective Leadership and Organizations

By

Russell Price

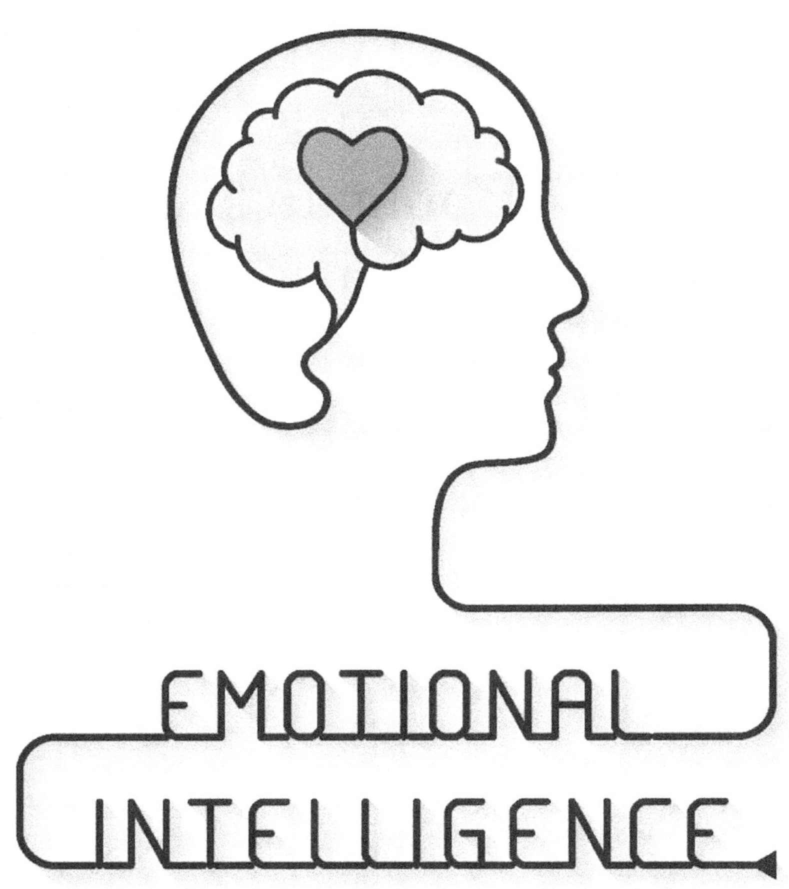

EMOTIONAL
INTELLIGENCE

befitting its nature, it is presented without assurance regarding its prolonged validity or interim quality. Trademarks that are mentioned are done without written consent and can in no way be considered an endorsement from the trademark holder.

Table of Contents

<u>VAGUS NERVE</u>

Overthinking

The Perfect Guide To Eliminate Negative Thoughts, Declutter Your mind, Focus On The Present and Start Thinking Positively

By

Russell Price

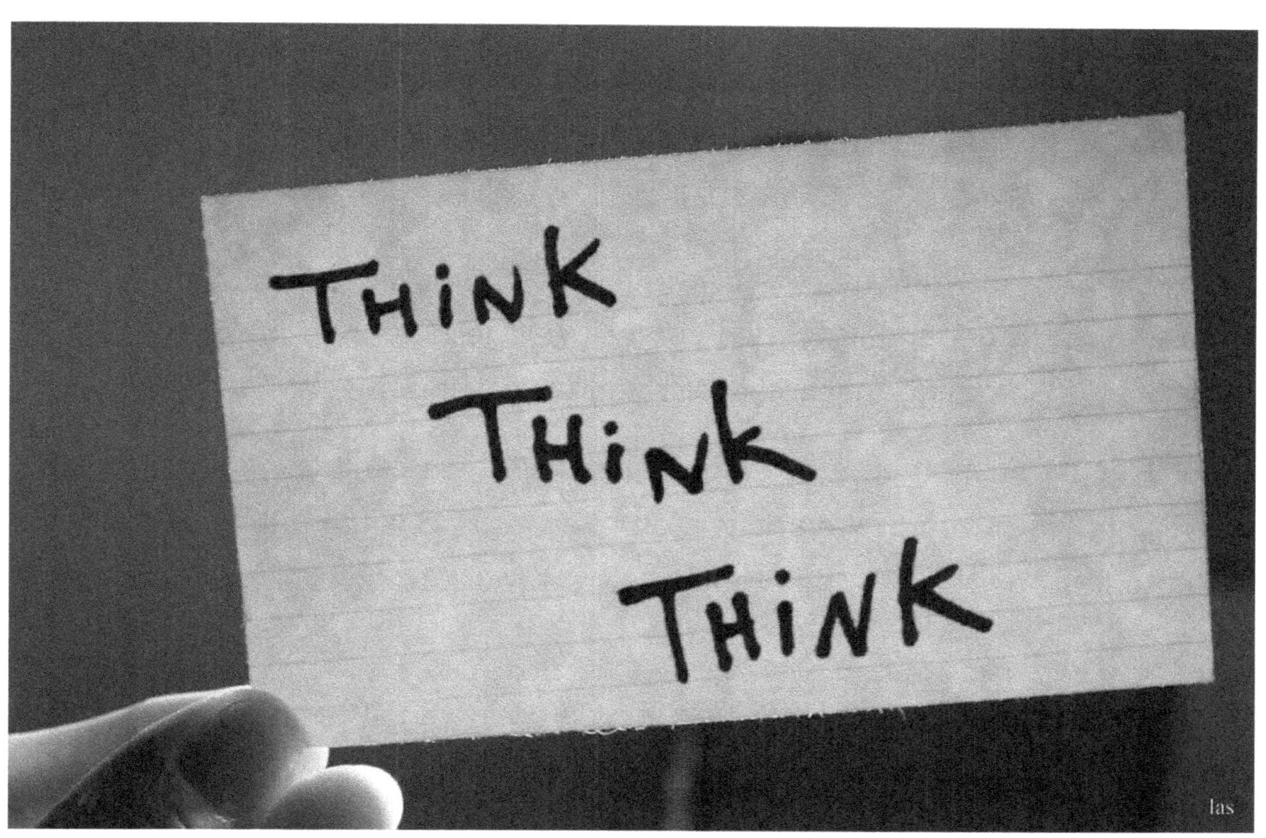

THINK
THINK
THINK
las

Introduction

It is effortless to fall into the device of overthinking about minor things throughout everyday life. So, when you are contemplating something, pose necessary inquiries to yourself. It has been found through an exploration that extending the viewpoint by utilizing these straightforward inquiries can snap you rapidly out of overthinking.

Endeavor to set brief time-limits for choices. So, figure out how to turn out to be better at settling on opportunities and to get a move on setting due dates in your everyday life. Regardless of when it is a little or a more excellent choice.

Be a person of movement. When you understand how in the first place making a move dependably, then you will wait less by overthinking. Setting due dates is one thing that will assist you with being a person of activity.

State stop in a condition where you understand you can't think straight. Now and again, when you are avaricious or when you are lying in bed and are going to rest, by the negative thoughts start murmuring around in your mind.

Do whatever it takes not to wind up stirred up in vague feelings of trepidation. Another snare that you have fallen into ordinarily that have impelled on overthinking is that you have lost all sense of direction in dubious feelings of fear about a circumstance in your life. Thus, your mind running wild has made fiasco situations about what could occur if you accomplish something. What is the most terrible that could happen? You ought to figure out how to pose this inquiry to yourself.

Invest the vast majority of your energy right now. Be right now in your regular day to day existence instead of before or a conceivable future.

Hinder how you do whatever you are doing well at this point. Move slower, talk slower, or ride your bike all the more gradually, for instance. By doing as such, you become increasingly mindful of how you utilize your body and what's going on surrounding you at present.

Endeavor to invest the more significant part of your energy with individuals who don't think more. Your social condition has considerable influence. Discover approaches to spend the more substantial portion of your energy and consideration with the general population and sources that effects affect your reasoning.

Countering Overthinking: Step Towards an Improved Life

So, suppose you're hanging about at a social event, encompassed by partners and customers, and you have spotted somebody you genuinely need to converse with. Perhaps it is business related, or you need to develop personal ties. How it is, you set up a psychological draft of what to state, as one does and means to meet them however a shivering apprehension in the back of your head leaves you speechless. Consider the possibility that they would prefer not to chat with you. Imagine a scenario where the specific line of discussion doesn't work out. Or then again even turns out badly? Your dread makes a kind of domino impact, and you start to think about the most terrible that could occur as the inescapable. With each idea, you are maneuvered further into the tangled wreckage of perplexity inside your psyche, and this, eventually, renders you unfit to try and talk any longer. You at that point, watch as someone else engages in discussion with the subject: an open door lost.

Overthinking and the resulting fretfulness and tension, while demonstrates to be a considerable hindrance in one's social and personal life, is additionally shockingly normal and for each person who is an injured individual to it, turns into the reason for circumstances lost and minutes that one would later lament. In any case, with a couple of day by day rehearses and a decoded frame of mind, it tends to be defeated effectively.

Acknowledgment

The initial move towards managing intemperate overthinking and tension is tolerating the issue in any case. Directly after this, would you have the option to feel free to settle it? In any case, while realizing that you are a remunerator is significant, it is likewise indispensable that you understand that you are not the only one in the circumstance and that there is no motivation to freeze. Overthinking is a common thing among many individuals today, and you would almost certainly beat it with an inspirational demeanor.

The best minute is the present minute.

One good precedent is relaxing. You'd be shocked at how much this makes a difference. Close your eyes and take full breaths for several minutes. Intently watching and taking full breaths help to pull you in the present minute and helps in clearing your head.

Another good precedent is reflecting on rehearsing care. The essential thought is to stay quiet and just spotlight on all that is around you intently, and this has done some incredible things for many individuals. Just once every day, close your eyes and attempt to take in the entirety of your environment. Tune in to your considerations; however, don't 'connect' with them, and inevitably, you can try to cut back their 'volume.'

Notwithstanding that, back off. Do all that you do with full consciousness of you doing it. Attempt and describe to yourself each progression that you make, and power yourself to see your environment. This will likewise assist you with staying right now.

Be certain

At the point when full to the overflow with confidence and liking yourself, you develop a positive outlook. You would end up to be less inclined to overthinking; thus, everything that you do or say ends up being improved. The first things you can do is get occupied. Structure an arrangement of what to accomplish for the afternoon and continue being profitable. Doing things shield your brain from straying, and notwithstanding that, completing stuff results in an extraordinary lift in certainty through a feeling of achievement. You ought to likewise attempt and accomplish something you're great at any rate once every day. Regardless of whether you're a specialist at playing an instrument or you have a remarkable ability for a computer game, take a break from your calendar and do it. It'll be an incredible assistance.

Another life-changing change you can make is to counterfeit it. This may sound hard, yet this works extraordinary. Imagine that you're a character you know, who is smart, intelligent, and sure about themselves. Maybe you know one from a TV program, a motion picture or a book. Feel free to convey all that you state with certainty, regardless of whether you don't know of it, or you're panicked. You'll see that as you counterfeit it to an ever-increasing extent, in the end, you acquire that trust, in actuality.

Give up

Endeavoring to control every one of incredible results is, without a doubt, the fundamental driver for compensation. Since when you do, you are likewise destined to hotly consider what to do in each snapshot of your life in dread of what could like this occur straightaway. The best thing you can do is to persuade yourself not to. Understand that you have nothing to do with what happens in your life, and thus, there is no motivation to stress over it. The universe has your destiny chosen, so you should make the most out of each minute. Attempt and understand this before anything you may falter do, and it'll assist you with stopping overthinking and take care of business.

Something else you can do make explicit time allotments to settle on any choice. Regardless of whether it is to proceed to converse with somebody or more significant life decisions which may constrain you to overthink. Pause for a moment for the little ones and a couple of days for the bigger ones in life and no more. This would push you to survey a choice usually and research to settle on the ideal decision. When you do decide on an opportunity, steel yourself and do what needs to be done. It may scare yet you'll see it remunerating toward the end.

By the day's end, the most significant piece to acknowledge is that we as a whole hold the possibility to accomplish all that we have longed for, and the main thing we need to do is to steel ourselves and evacuate our hindrances. What's more, that has a significant effect.

Managing Life and Overthinking

After all the diligent work, this ought to be the season when we at long last quit worrying and begin having fun. How would you stop those annoying 'imagine a scenario where?' stresses are swarming back.

We as a whole do it once in a while - stress over things we've said or done, examine disposable remarks others have or invest hours dismembering the significance of a specific email or letter. Nearly without acknowledging it, we get sucked into a winding of negative contemplations and feelings that take our delight and excitement. It's an example that a few clinicians bring over reasoning. The underlying considerations lead to progressively negative musings, the inquiries to more inquiries. The over reasoning turns into a course that matures and fabricates so that everything gains out of power. Stall out in this negative cycle, and it can influence your life. It can likewise prompt some downright awful choices when generally little issues turn out to be so dramatically overemphasized that you lose your point of view on them.

When we over think-focusing on what has occurred previously (future) - we are obliterating the minute we are in. You pass up encountering and appreciating the present time and place of your life.

For what reason do we do it? - At the most fundamental dimension, the science of our cerebrum makes it simple to overthink. Musings and recollections don't merely sit in our cerebrums segregated and free from one another - they are woven together in mind-boggling systems of affiliations. One consequence of all these perplexing interconnections is that musings concerning a specific issue in your life can trigger considerations about other associated problems.

A large portion of us has some negative recollections, stresses over the future, or worries about the present. A significant part of the time we're most likely not aware of these negative musings. In any case, when they come over us, regardless of whether it's because the climate's terrible or because we alcoholic an excessive amount of wine, it's simpler to review the negative recollections and start the cycle of over reasoning. Numerous ladies are over-burden with juggling home and work responsibilities and want to do everything superbly. We will, in general feel in charge of everybody, a figure we ought to be in charge and set ourselves strangely particular requirements.

How to defeat it? - If you're endless over scholar, just being advised to invest significant time and unwind won't do it for you. You have to find a way to control and conquer contrary reasoning. Ending the propensity isn't simple, and there's no enchantment answer for everybody, except these are a portion of the means that specialists propose can enable you to break out of the negative cycle of over reasoning.

1. Offer yourself a reprieve - Free your brain with something that draws in your fixation and lifts your mindset - regardless of whether it's perusing a decent book, strolling the canine, having a back rub or doing the rec center.

2. Take yourself close by - When you see yourself going over similar musings, let yourself know immovably to stop — post yellow stickers around your work area and the house as updates.

3. Jettison the postponing strategies - If there are specific circumstances or spots that trigger over reasoning, for example, a work area heaped high with papers or open letters or messages, at that point take care of business, anyway little. Over reasoning that is connected with inertia can turn into an endless loop. Rather than living in dread of what you can't do and what could occur, it's far superior to handle it virtually by accomplishing something.

4. Discharge your contemplations - Issues that expect large extents after frantic stressing can all of a sudden dissolve away when you talk them through with a companion. They can appear to be absurd or even amusing. Making a joke out of them can genuinely defuse your stresses.

5. Plan for deduction time - choose when you enable yourself to think. Point of confinement the time you give yourself and adhere to your timetable. Envision keeping every one of those contemplations in a single box that you can take out at a specific time, at that point seal and put it away when the time runs out.

6. Appreciate the occasion - Actively plan things that you understand. It doesn't make a difference what it is - whatever works for you. It's difficult to grieve in negative over reasoning when you're having some good times.

7. Express your feelings - Instead of going into a profound examination of what your feelings truly mean, enable yourself to encounter them for a change. Sob, shout, punch a pad, will allow yourself to feel the warmth and after that proceed onward.

8. Pardon yourself - That doesn't mean imagining that slight or harmful comments never occurred, yet it means settling on a decision to set them aside as opposed to harp on them.

9. Be careful - Take time every day to be at the time. It won't be simple, however, persevere, and you'll receive the benefits. Go out in the greenhouse to watch the dusk, go through 15 minutes in the recreation center at noon or sit in a bistro all alone. Try not to exile the considerations, let them travel every which way, yet see what's near and how your body feels

Chapter 1.　　What is Overthinking?

There are many ways of describing overthinking. It can be understood as a situation where one cannot stop worrying and thinking about things. Overthinking is not a disorder. It involves a fear that grows in you and overwhelms you, but you can't help yourself but let it do so. In some cases, instead of crying it out, you simply opt to hold back your tears. It's the fear of failure: failing at your job, failing a certain class, failing in your relationships. Overthinking drives you to work hard for unrealistic expectations. This might sound productive, but in reality, you will be exhausted by maintaining this pace. Thinking too much leads to exhaustion. Emotionally and physically, you will feel exhausted since your mind never stops. It is always flooded with thoughts and the worst thing about it is that you believe there is nothing you can do.

Overthinking is that inner voice that tries to bring you down. It criticizes you and destroys your confidence and self-esteem. You not only doubt yourself, but you also doubt those who are close to you. It pushes you to second guess everything. Thinking too much can be compared to a spreading fire. It burns down everything that it finds on its way. Therefore, you will suffer as a result of overthinking.

Overthinking is when your mind clings to the faults that you have made and takes you through them throughout the day. When you overthink, your life will be on constant pause. You will always feel as though you are waiting for the right moment to do something. The problem is that this moment never arrives. You're always anticipating that something could go wrong. You will be overly careful when doing anything. This is influenced by the fact that you are just worried things might not work out as expected.

The following are clear indications that you think too much. You might try to deny it, but consider these signs and question yourself whether these are some of the things that you might have experienced.

You Overanalyze Everything

If you notice that you overanalyze everything around you, then you are certainly an overthinker. This means that you may try to find a deeper meaning in all the experiences that you go through. When meeting new people, instead of engaging in productive communication, you may focus instead on how other people perceive you. Someone could be giving you a particular look and you may make several assumptions just based on that look. Overthinking consumes you. You end up wasting a lot of energy trying to figure out and make sense of the world around you. What you don't realize is that not everything has intrinsic meaning.

You Think Too Much, But Don't Act

An overthinker will be affected by something called analysis paralysis. This is a scenario where you think too much about something, but don't do anything about it in the end. In this case, you spend a lot of time weighing the options you have at your disposal. At first, you make up your mind on what the best alternative might be. Later, you compare your decision to other possible decisions that you could take. This means that you can't stop thinking about the possibilities and whether or not you made the right decision. Ultimately, you end up not making a decision. You only find yourself in a vicious circle where you simply think a lot, but there is little that you do. Perhaps the best strategy to prevent yourself from falling into a thinking trap is to try out the alternatives you have. A simple decision to act will make a huge difference.

You Can't Let Go

Often, we make erroneous decisions that could lead us to fail. When this happens, it can be daunting to let go more so when you reflect on the sacrifices you have made to get to the point you are at. You might feel that it is painful to let go after you have invested a lot of money on a certain business. The issue here is that you don't want to fail. However, it is important to realize that failing to let go only holds you back from trying out something else that could work. It also affects your life since you will think repeatedly about your failures. You need to move on. It's important that you shift your attention to something else instead of beating yourself up over something that is now out of your control. Convince yourself that there is nothing you can do about what has already happened apart from learning from it. The best thing you can do is to let go and move on.

You Always Want to Know Why

Without a doubt, the notion of asking why can be helpful to solve problems. This is because this probing attitude gets you the answers that you might be looking for. Nonetheless, it can also be damaging when you can't help but always wonder why. Normally, we are accustomed to answering questions from kids. They just love to ask why about anything and everything. They will not hesitate to ask you why you don't talk to your neighbor. Why children are born or simply why you love to walk. There's something unique about how children are curious. Overthinkers maintain such investigative attitude throughout their lives. As adults, there are certain things that only have surface meanings. Therefore, probing too much can only affect how other people see you.

You Analyze People

The way you see other people can also say a lot about you. In most cases, you get lost thinking too much about how other people behave. You may tend to judge everybody that you come across. This one walks in a funny way. That person is not dressed well. You wonder what someone sitting at the park is smiling about. When these thoughts fill your head, you will only drain yourself. Spending too much time focusing on other people will only deter you from using your mind productively. Instead of visualizing your goals and your future, you waste your energy mulling over little things that add no value to you.

Regular Insomnia

Do you find it hard to sleep sometimes? You may get worked up over the idea that your brain cannot shut down and stop thinking. Sadly, this can paralyze you since your brain doesn't get the rest that it deserves. Gradually, you will notice a decrease in your productivity. You are unlikely to feel good about yourself since there is little that you achieve. Worrying too much about not being able to sleep can make you uneasy and you may find yourself in a state of captivity. If this is something that you have been experiencing, then it sounds like you might be an overthinker. What could you do about this? First, if you are not active, then it is vital that you find a way of keeping yourself busy. In addition, meditation is a great practice that can help you stop overthinking and relax and focus on the present.

You Always Live in Fear

Are you afraid about what the future has in store for you? If you answer yes to this question, then chances are that you're caged in your mind. Living in fear could drive you to resort to drugs and alcohol as your best remedy.

You will gain the perception that by taking drugs, it will help you drown your sorrows and help you forget. Unfortunately, this is not the case since drugs and alcohol are mere depressants. They slow down your brain functioning. As a result, you tend to believe that they are helping you forget.

You're Always Fatigued

Do you always wake up in the morning feeling tired? This could be a result of stress or depression. Instead of living a productive life, you find yourself waking up late, tired, and unmotivated. The reason why this happens is because you don't give your mind an opportunity to rest. It has been working day and night. In the evening, instead of sleeping you find yourself awake all night because you are overthinking. Your mind cannot work for 24 hours straight at the same level of functioning. You will only suffer from burnouts. You need to give your mind ample time to rest and reboot.

You Don't Live in the Present

Do you find it difficult to enjoy life? Why do you think you find it daunting to sit back, relax, and be happy with your friends? The mere fact that you can't stay in the present implies that you won't focus on what is happening in the present. Overthinking will blind you from noticing anything good that is currently happening around you. You will often think about the worst that can happen. The issue is that you are trapped in your mind and there is nothing outside your thoughts that you can constructively think about.

Failure to live in the present denies you the opportunity to improve relationships with other people. In fact, you will live in fear that they will criticize you. Therefore, you will only want to exist in your cocoon. Again, this will lead to stress.

There are different forms of overthinking that could affect the quality of the decisions we make. Common forms of overthinking are succinctly discussed in the following paragraphs.

Abstract Thinking

This refers to a form of thinking which goes beyond concrete realities. For instance, when you are trying to formulate theories to explain your observations, then you're engaging in abstract thinking. When your business is not performing well, you might jump to the conclusion that it's because of the economy.

Complexity

The complexity form of overthinking comes about when there are many factors to consider in your decision-making process. In this case, these numerous factors could prevent you from weighing the true importance of each one of them. The effect is that it could prevent you from making decisions promptly.

Avoidance

Avoidance occurs when one tries to avoid doing something by using the decision-making process as their excuse.

Cold Logic

When using cold logic to think, you tend to avoid relying on human factors, including language, culture, personality, emotion, and social dynamics. The outcome is that you end up making biased decisions that do not consider legal or social realities.

Intuition Neglect

This occurs when one fails to consider what they already know. In other words, one opts to overthink something that they already know a thing or two about. Instead of following your gut instinct, you overthink and end up making the wrong decisions.

Creating Problems

You may also find yourself thinking in a way where you are creating problems that are not there in the first place. There are certain situations or things which are not as complex as you think. In ordinary situations, it would have taken you a minute or two to solve them. It is vital to focus more on the bigger picture and not nitpick at the details. Sometimes it is important to see things as they are. Don't complicate your life by thinking of potential problems.

Magnifying the Issue

Usually, small problems require simple solutions. There are instances where we amplify these problems and we end up coming up with overly complex solutions to solve them. This is another form of overthinking. You end up wasting your resources to come up with huge solutions that don't match the problems you are experiencing.

Fear of Failure

Fear of failure is not a new concept to most people. In fact, this is what motivates most of us to work hard. Instead of working hard for a bright future, you find yourself drawing motivation from the fear you have developed inside you.

Irrelevant Decisions

There are times when we make irrelevant decisions because we force ourselves to make these decisions, yet we are not required to make them. For instance, when thinking about our future, there are instances where we end up making irrelevant decisions based on assumptions.

Getting married, for example, based on the assumptions you have, you might conclude that you need to get married because you're getting old.

Causes of Overthinking

After looking at the possible signs that could indicate you are an overthinker and the types of overthinking, it is important to reflect on the causes. While reading through this section, ask yourself: what causes you to overthink? Frankly, depending on the situation that you might be going through, there are varying reasons why you may think too much. For instance, your fear of embarrassment could push you to overthink what you should wear or how you should present yourself in front of other people. On the other hand, the fear of failure can lead you to work hard towards achieving your goals.

The following are common reasons why you may overthink.

Lack of Confidence

Lack of confidence is one of the main reasons why people tend to overthink. When you're not sure about what to do, it opens doors for uncertainty. Your mind is filled with fear as a result. It is worth noting that you can never be sure about the decisions that you make. Accordingly, there are times when you will be required to take risks when making important decisions. Taking such risks prevents you from torturing your mind since you will be acting without spending too much time thinking. Deciding to do something gives you confidence. This will have an impact on how you handle problems in your life. With time, you will develop into more of a decision maker than a thinker.

Second-Guessing Yourself

Still on the issue of confidence, doubting yourself is mentally exhausting. Sure, it is understandable that you may make the wrong decisions. No one is perfect, so don't expect that you will always make the right choices. However, constantly being indecisive will rob you of your confidence. The main issue here is that you will frequently stress yourself over anything that requires you to make a choice.

To avoid second-guessing yourself, it is crucial that you trust your abilities. This will be helpful as you will become more self-aware and in turn, end up making sound decisions. The exciting thing is that you will avoid the notion of repeatedly asking other people for their opinions before doing anything.

Being a Constant Worrier

Research shows that severe anxiety is a widespread issue among American teenagers. Most of them are afraid that they might fail in their lives. In addition, they always worry too much about the world around them. As a result, it is not surprising that they tend to worry about what others think about them. The habit of constantly worrying that things could go wrong will push you to overthink. The images that you develop in your mind will mostly feature the thoughts of failing. Frankly, this drains energy from you.

Instead of worrying too much about the future, you should understand that thinking positively and constructively about how to accomplish your goals is more productive. Remember, the future is uncertain to everybody. No one knows what will happen tomorrow. Therefore, the best thing that you can do about the future is to plan for it. Changing your mentality to focus more on the goals you have set and how you can achieve them will motivate you to live a life with a sense of direction. The best part is that the sense of optimism you develop will help you see life from a positive perspective.

Overthinking Acts as Protection

You might find yourself thinking too much because it is a way of safeguarding yourself from your life's troubles. The reality is that you are afraid to take action. Therefore, overthinking only thwarts your progress in life. You will only be held captive by your thoughts. It is worth realizing that it is beneficial to act even when you're not sure about yourself.

Consider the benefits you gain from the experiences you face in your life. These experiences make you stronger. You will be more aware of the pros and cons of engaging in certain activities since you have experienced them. Avoid falling for the idea that overthinking will protect you from your problems. It's better to face your challenges head-on.

You Cannot Relax

It will be difficult for your mind to stop thinking if you pay too much attention to the problem that you are facing. Your problems will put you in a state of constant tension. The worst thing is that you haven't invested your time in learning how to relax. For that reason, it will be difficult to eliminate negative thoughts from your mind. Individuals who value the importance of working out or meditating and engaging in yoga exercises can prevent their minds from overthinking. Meditation works to help you connect your mind and body. Therefore, through this self-awareness, you can identify the existence of negative thoughts and learn how to separate yourself from them.

You Yearn for Perfection

Being a perfectionist might be perceived as a good thing at first. However, there is a huge price to pay to live as a perfectionist. Often, you will want everything to fall into place just like you want it. You will never be satisfied with anything that comes up short of what you had anticipated. Therefore, this means that you will always overthink about what needs to be done. Your mind will be in a constant loop of overthinking things, whether they are done in the right way or not. Developing such a habit will only cause detrimental effects to both your mental and physical health.

Chapter 2.   Declutter Your Mind

We live in a world that requires us to act on many things. Besides overcoming daily stressors, we should learn how to develop the right habits that prevent us from worrying and thinking negative thoughts. The strenuous environment and the hustle and bustle we have to face often fills our minds with clutter. It often reaches a point where our minds can't stop thinking. You may become overwhelmed with thoughts which leaves your mind in a total mess. Does this sound like you? If yes, then your mind is waving a white flag at you and may require some decluttering.

In the same way that you will regularly spare some time to declutter your office and your house, the mind also requires decluttering. This will guarantee that you free up some space for optimal functioning. However, it is not as easy as it sounds since you cannot see exactly what is in the mind. As a result, the cleaning process will be different from the normal decluttering that you have been used to. So, how do you empty out the unnecessary from your mind? This chapter will focus on answering this question and it will help you understand the significance of decluttering your mind.

Causes of Mental Clutter

In an ordinary case, when cleaning your home or office, you will start by identifying the items that are causing clutter. Likewise, before decluttering your mind, it is important that you start by identifying the causes of mental clutter. The importance of doing this is that it guarantees that you can effectively deal with clutter in the long run. You will be more aware of the factors that contribute to clutter in your mind and work to avoid them.

The following are some of the common causes of mental clutter.

Overwhelm

Naturally, if you are overwhelmed with things, then it will lead to disorder in your mind. As a result, it will be daunting for you to establish a reasonable way of dealing with your issues. This causes clutter. Fortunately, you can overcome this by acknowledging the fact that you can't handle everything at once. This means that you should break down your tasks into smaller, yet manageable mini-tasks. Handle these things one at a time. At the end of the day, you will realize that there is a lot that you have accomplished without feeling overwhelmed.

Over-Commitment

Committing yourself to finish certain activities on your to-do list is a good thing. Nonetheless, when you can't say no to other assignments, it means that you are over-committing yourself. Handling too many things will only lead to frustration. This is because there is a probability that you might fail to deliver. Learning to say no is an essential attribute of living a productive life. Saying no shouldn't be considered a bad thing since you're committing yourself to work productively on what you can manage. So, avoid over-committing yourself and taking on more than you can handle.

Fear

If you're afraid to let go of what has happened in the past, then are likely to strain your mind. The habit of holding on to things and thoughts often consumes us. Instead of working productively, your mind will keep ruminating on the past. This is pure clutter. Why should you put yourself through this torture when you can simply learn to let go?

Emotional Overload

Maybe your mind is filled with unwanted thoughts and feelings that keep draining energy from you. For instance, you might be dealing with a looming family crisis and it ends up affecting your productivity at work. If this is what you are going through, then it is best that you find time to deal with the issue. Ask for a leave of absence and free your mind from having to think over this matter repeatedly.

Lack of Time

Time will always be a prevalent issue. In everything that you do, you will often feel as though you don't have enough time. The reality is that there is enough time to handle all the important things in your life if you prioritize and plan effectively. Therefore, you shouldn't use the excuse that you lack time. The only issue here is that you may not know how to effectively manage your time. Organize yourself and prioritize what needs to be done first. This way, you will have more time to handle pending tasks on your to-do list.

Procrastination

If you are a victim of procrastination, then it comes as no surprise that your mind is always in a state of overdrive. Pushing things to be done at a later time means that there is a lot that will require your attention when 'later' comes. After a while, you will feel overwhelmed that you cannot complete everything on time. The problem began with the decision to procrastinate.

A Major Change in Life

Another reason why your mind might be filled with clutter is because of a major change which has occurred in your life. Frankly, sometimes we have to acknowledge the fact that change is inevitable. People fail to embrace change in their lives. As a result, they spend too much time doing what they used to do instead of changing. When faced with such predicaments, it is imperative that you evaluate what's going on in your life and strive to change.

Familiarity with the causes of mental clutter is the first step towards successful mental decluttering. Once you are aware of what causes clutter in your mind, you can develop practical solutions of how to get rid of them. It is worth bearing in mind that in most cases, there are multiple reasons why your mind is cluttered. So, open up your mind when trying to identify the factors that cause your messy mental state.

Practical Tips on How to Declutter Your Mind

Now that you understand what's causing all the clutter, let's look at some of the ways in which you can declutter your mind.

Set Priorities

Sometimes we fail to realize that a life without goals is a boring life. Living a goalless life is like wandering in the forest forever without a map. You don't have a particular destination that you want to reach. What's worse, you don't even know how to maneuver through the forest. Similarly, life without goals has no meaning. Your daily activities will be consumed with people and activities that don't add value to you. You will live in your comfort zone since there is nothing that you're actually targeting to achieve.

Setting priorities is a good place to start when looking to declutter your mind. This requires that you sit down and identify things that matter the most to your life. List down these goals and work to ensure that your actions are in line with the set goals. Setting priorities create structure with your to-do lists. You will begin to value the importance of delegating tasks when you feel like you can't handle them. More importantly, you will learn to say no since you comprehend the significance of handling only what you value and what you can take on.

Keep a Journal

Keeping a journal is a great strategy to help organize your thoughts. People tend to underestimate the power of noting down their thoughts every day. Journaling helps you rid your mind from things that you might not be aware of. It enhances your working memory and also guarantees that you can effectively manage stress. Similarly, the habit of noting down your daily experiences in a journal helps you express your emotions that may be bottled up within you. Therefore, you create space to experience new things in life. The effect of this is that you can relieve yourself from the anxiety that you might have been experiencing.

Learn to Let Go

Decluttering your mind can also be made easier if you learn to let go. Holding on to things in the past adds little or no value to your life. In fact, it only affects your emotional and mental wellbeing. The mere fact that you cannot let go implies that you will find it daunting to look ahead. Your mind will stagnate and this will stress you out. If you were a bird and you wanted to fly, what would you do? Without a doubt, you would want to free yourself from any burden that weighs you down. Apply this to real life and free yourself from any emotional baggage that you might be holding on to. Whether it's your failed past relationships or failed job opportunities, just let go. There is a greater reward in letting go since you open doors for new opportunities in your life.

Breathe

Breathing exercises would also be helpful in clearing clutter from your mind. There are certain forms of meditation that depend on breathing exercises to focus your attention on the breath. So, how do you practice breathing exercises? Start by taking a slow deep breath. Pause for a moment before exhaling. While breathing in and out, focus your mind on how you are breathing. Concentrate on how your breath goes in and out of your nose. It's relaxing, right? Practicing breathing exercises more often relaxes your mind. Besides helping you to relax, it boosts your immune system in profound ways. More about this will be discussed later in Chapter 6.

Declutter Your Physical Environment

If you live in a messy house, then there is a good chance that you're more likely frustrated. This may be because you find it difficult to find things you need. For instance, you end up wasting a lot of time looking for your car keys before heading to work. This affects how you start your day. You will be stressed that you arrived late and that there are numerous tasks waiting for you. Therefore, decluttering your physical space will also have a positive impact on your mind. Keeping things organized also means that your mind is virtually organized to handle the things that ought to be handled.

Learn to Share Your Thoughts

There is an overall positive feeling when you sit down to share your feelings with someone you care about. Instead of holding back your tears and emotions, sharing your feelings with your loved ones can clear emotional clutter from your mind. Have you ever wondered why you can think more clearly after sharing your sad feelings with another person? There is power in sharing your thoughts and feelings with other people. You can be more certain that you are making informed decisions since your mind can think clearly without being blinded by your emotions.

Curb Your Information Intake

The information that we consume affects the quality of the decisions we make. Unfortunately, the information we consume is sometimes unimportant to our lives. It only fills our minds with clutter and this prevents us from thinking clearly and making the right decisions. The worst thing is that it causes anxiety and stress as we tend to worry about the worst that could happen to us after what we have read or watched over the internet. Limiting what you consume from the internet can help prevent unwanted information from taking up space in your mind. So, instead of starting your day by checking your social media page, consider going for a walk or reading a book. The point here is that you should substitute your unproductive time on the internet by doing productive things.

Spare Some Time to Unwind

More importantly, to declutter your mind, you should consider taking a break. You might believe that taking breaks is unproductive, but the truth is that your productivity can be given a huge boost when you take breaks more often. Giving yourself some time to unwind helps you recharge. As a result, you end up doing more in less time. This is what effectiveness and efficiency are all about. They both account for your productivity.

The Importance of Decluttering Your Mind

Decluttering the physical space around you will help you create more space for more important things. In addition, such tidiness will also have an impact on your mind since everything will be organized and you will know where everything is. There are few things reminding you that they need to be arranged. Likewise, decluttering your mind also has its benefits.

A Decrease in Stress and Anxiety

Clutter will stress you out. Feeling like your mind is messy may make you feel tired since there is a lot to do yet so little time. Similarly, mental clutter will also make you feel unconfident. You will rarely be confident about your abilities. Repeatedly, you will notice that you second-guess everything that you do. All this is happening because your mind can't think straight. There is a lot that it is focusing on and therefore, finding practical solutions to the little things ahead of you may seem impossible.

By using the recommended strategies discussed herein to clear clutter from your mind, you can be more equipped to lower your stress and anxiety levels. Your mind will feel more liberated. The new space that you have created will give your mind the energy it needs to think and make smart decisions. As a result, you will feel more confident about yourself and the decisions that you make.

An Improvement in Your Productivity

Clutter can prevent your mind from achieving the focus it needs to handle the priorities that you have set for yourself. For instance, instead of waking up early and working on an important project, you might find yourself paying too much attention to the emotional burden that is weighing you down. Frankly, this thwarts your level of productivity. You are unlikely to use your time wisely, which affects your productivity.

Eliminating unwanted thoughts and emotions will help you focus more on what is important. You will find it easier to set priorities and work towards them. You will wake up feeling motivated and goal-oriented. In the short run, you will notice an improvement in your efficiency. Over time, you will realize that you're more effective than ever before since there is more that you can do in less time.

Enhanced Emotional Intelligence

There are numerous situations in which we allow our emotions to affect how we perceive things in life. One minute you love someone and the next minute you think that they are the worst and you regret ever meeting them. In addition, these emotions cloud our judgment and we end up making conclusions that are not valid. In most cases, this occurs when there is a lot on our minds that we have to handle. The result is that we fail to deal with these emotions in an effective manner.

Decluttering your mind requires that you get rid of negative thoughts that would lead to negative emotions. As a result, decluttering more often implies that you will master how to deal with negative feelings. You are less likely to allow negative feelings to weigh you down. This is because you understand that they are just emotions and letting them go is the best course of action you can take.

You can transform your life by choosing to declutter your mind. You will end up making better decisions that lead your life in the right direction. However, it is important to note that the decluttering process will only be successful if you know where the clutter is coming from. To start, you can evaluate yourself and find out why there is so much clutter in your mind. Is it because you overcommit yourself? Is it because you are overwhelmed with the challenges that you have to handle? Is it caused by your fear of making mistakes? Knowing the reasons for clutter ensures that you can control clutter in the long haul. In addition, the digital age that we're living in should not be an excuse to fill your mind with unwanted information. Feed your mind with quality information that drives you to achieve your goals. Curb your information intake and free yourself from clutter.

Chapter 3.   Challenging your Thoughts

To stop overthinking, you need to first retrain your brain. Fortunately, there are many exercises and activities that you can use to reshape the way you think.

Now that you know a little about overthinking, and you also know when you are on the verge of dropping into that deep whirlpool of infinite negative emotions, you can start getting rid of it entirely, and you can start by challenging your thoughts before they run out of control.

Before You Begin

Here are some of the things that you need to know before you start challenging your negative thoughts so you will not get too surprised and overwhelmed with everything that is happening.

1. You need to know that challenging your thoughts might feel unnatural, sometimes even forced at first. But with a bit of practice, it will start to feel natural and believable.

2. To build up your confidence for thought challenging, you should practice them on thoughts that are not as upsetting and provides a bit more flexibility. It is also a good idea to practice this technique when you are still feeling a bit neutral and not too overwhelmed by your thoughts. Trying to practice thought challenging after a particularly rough and problematic day would be asking too much from yourself.

3. The first couple of times you try thought challenging it would be best if you jot down your responses. Often, when beginners try doing it in their heads, they end up with their thoughts going around in

circles, which makes their thoughts all the more intense, and might cause them to spiral into overthinking.

4. Another benefit of taking down notes is that if a similar thought pops up in the future, you can refer to your notes and find out how you reacted to it.

5. You can practice with a family member or a friend whom you know will not judge you. Practicing with another person might help you by shedding light on the blind spots of your thinking, or they can offer you different viewpoints that you might find useful.

6. When you are first practicing thought challenging, you should focus on a single thought instead of a series of them this early in the game. For instance, instead of thinking "It's pretty obvious that my bosses thought I messed up the project" you should break down your thoughts into smaller, simpler sentences, and then challenge these thoughts one by one. You will only be confusing yourself if you start challenging a pile of thoughts at the same time.

7. Do something that will distract yourself once you finish working through a couple of thought challenging questions. This will give you some time for your mind to settle down.

Now that you know what you should expect, here are some of the most popular thought challenging exercise that you can try now.

Step Back and Assess the Situation

Here's a scenario that you might have experienced: you feel as if your boss is constantly and intentionally ignoring you. You think that the reason why your boss did not greet you this morning is because you somehow messed up something and that he is contemplating on firing you very soon. Usually, this kind of thoughts will cause your mind to overthink and cause you to lose sleep, thus causing you to not be as efficient at work, which therefore leads to you getting fired; in short, overthinking problems turns them into self-fulfilling prophecies.

On the other hand, if you just step back and analyze your thoughts before your overactive brain blows it way out of proportion, you can control it better. In the case mentioned above, remind yourself that your boss rarely greets anyone at all, and whatever screw up you might have made during the past couple of days is not grounds for your termination. Next, think about what you could do in order to not get fired, like increasing your productivity, or maybe learn a new skill that can help you do your job better.

In just a couple of minutes, you have derailed your train of negative thought before it even gets a chance to gain momentum.

Write Them All Down

Another way to challenge your negative thoughts before they trigger you to overthink is to write them all down on a piece of paper. When you write down the things that are bothering you, it gives them a somewhat tangible form, which actually helps you reanalyze them in a more rational manner. If you want to take this to the next level, you can start making a thought journal.

What is a thought journal/diary?

A thought diary is different from the traditional form of journaling, it has a structure that you have to follow to make analyzing your thoughts much easier. For instance, in a thought diary, you do not start an entry with a

"Dear Diary" or any form of it, the entries look more like a ledger if anything.

You make a thought diary by making a couple of columns on the page and then you title them as follows:

Antecedent – These are the things that triggered you during the day.

Beliefs – These are your thoughts about the things that you listed in the first column.

Consequences – These are the things that happened because of your thoughts.

This is why a thought journal is called an ABC journal.

Here is an example on how you write an entry in your thought journal. You suddenly start worrying because you have an upcoming bill that you have to pay, this is your consequence. On the second column, you write that you were worried because you might not be able to make your due date. On the trigger section, you could write that you were watching the evening news when you suddenly remembered that you needed to pay.

After some time of writing in your thoughts journal, you might start noticing that the triggers are usually not related to the thoughts that made you worry. Thoughts just occur, and the triggers that caused them to surface might be related to them at all; thoughts are fickle in that way.

In the consequences column, you then might write down something like, "I took an aspirin to get rid of the headache that I felt was coming."

Every Sunday evening you could review your entries and then think of the things that you could have done better. For instance, for the entry above, instead of taking an aspirin, you could have just walked around the park to clear your mind, or at the very least you could have eaten an apple or something just so your headache will not get any worse. Or you could call your utility company and inform them that you might be a little late on the payment, but you will be paying, and ask if it is possible for them to waive the late fees. Your thought diary will help you make sense of your muddled thoughts by laying them out on paper for you to easily analyze. This tool can help you understand your less-than-ideal coping skills and why you end up making choices that lead to consequences that are not really best for you. With the help of a thought journal you can change your future consequences by restating and reanalyzing your past thoughts and making the necessary adjustments.

Benefits of a thought diary

Writing in a thought journal/diary helps you identify the things that trigger you into overthinking. When you write down your thoughts, you will easily see if they are actually legitimate concerns, or if they are just irrational. Thought journals help you recall how you behaved during the time you were triggered into overthinking, and in time you will start to notice the patterns in the way you think.

When you recognize your existing thought patterns, it will be possible for you to change not only your behavior, but also your thoughts. When you notice evil thoughts start to creep in, you can practice mindfulness (more on this later) and just observe and acknowledge them so they will go away. You actually do not need to behave according to your thoughts, you can actually ignore them and just continue living your own life. It is much better to write down "I ignored the thought of…" instead of "I went to the pub and drank a few pints to make myself forget", and if you notice that you are doing basically the same thing almost every day then your thought diary is actually working.

Make a habit of writing a thought journal

It is highly advisable that you make a habit out of writing down your thoughts using the format mentioned above. You can use a small notebook, a stack of papers, anything that you can write on and keep confidential. No one else aside from you and your therapist (if you are seeing one) must know about the existence of this journal; no one else should have access to your inner thoughts.

If you do not want to use the traditional method, you can also use your smartphone or laptop to create a secret document. Gradually over time, you will start noticing when you are starting to spiral into overthinking and then stop yourself from going any further.

Negative emotions, like those that shatter your confidence to pieces, can usually lead to clinical depression, makes you feel irrationally lonely, hopeless, and they will break you apart from the inside. Writing helps you get rid of your self-destructive thoughts. It is an art that can help you share your innermost feelings and your deepest thoughts.

Writing down your feelings onto paper is a way for you to freely express your views and opinions on the things that happened during the day, and what effect they had on your life. You are not just writing words on paper, you are effectively eliminating all these negative thoughts from your mind, and with them goes all that negativity that came with them.

Get a Hobby

Have you always wanted to learn to play the piano, the guitar, ukulele, or any other kind of musical instrument, why not try learning today? Do you want to get good at drawing, calligraphy, or painting? Attend classes or watch online video tutorials. You can also play your favorite video games for an hour or so. Having a hobby not only gives you a creative outlet, they also provide you with a way to create something with your hands, it also allows you to think individually, and most importantly, hobbies provide you with an escape from your negative thoughts.

Whenever you feel as if your thoughts are starting to overwhelming you, whip out your hobby kit, and immerse yourself in the activity. Lose yourself in the skills, coordination, concentration, and repetition that your hobby requires you to do. Focus your mind on the comfort or challenge brought about by your chosen hobby, and allow it to chase away all of the worries that used to trigger your overthinking.

Meditate Your Worries Away

Meditation can actually help you focus your mind away from the things that are troubling you. In fact, guided meditation can help you reset your mind, thus leaving you unburdened, and refreshed; ready for all the challenges that may come your way.

Meditation is different from mindfulness; the latter is a spur of the moment technique that you can use anywhere and anytime. Meditation, in the purest sense, should be practiced in a calm, silent, and relaxing environment as much as possible.

Here are a couple of meditation techniques. Give them all a try and choose the one that you vibe the most with.

1. Focused breathing

Breathing is one of the body's involuntary actions, meaning you do not really need to command your body to breath, it just happens. However, you can turn your breathing into a form of meditation just by taking notice of every breath that you take.

In focused breathing meditation, you take long, slow, deep breaths; breaths so deep that you fill your abdomen with air as well. To practice this form of meditation, you disengage your mind from all thoughts, and focus all your attention on your breathing. This is especially helpful for when you start noticing that your thoughts are starting to go out of your control.

However, this technique might not be appropriate for those who have respiratory ailments, like asthma and some heart ailments.

2. Guided Meditation

This technique requires you to come up with soothing scenery, places, or experiences that might help you relax better. If you have difficulty thinking up scenes for your guided meditation sessions, you can use any one of the many free apps available online.

Guided imagery is great because you just need to follow the instructions of the smooth voiced instructor and you will be alright. This technique is best for those who suffer from chronic intrusive thoughts.

3. Mindfulness Meditation

As mentioned earlier, this is different from actual meditation. This practice require only that you are sitting comfortably, and then focusing on the present without drifting towards your troubling thoughts of the past and the future. This form is presently enjoying quite a surge of popularity mainly because it can help people who are struggling with anxiety, chronic pain, and depression.

4. Yoga, Tai Chi, or Qui Gong

These three ancient arts might not seem similar, however, they all combine rhythmic breathing with different postures and body movements. The fact that you have to focus on your breathing while engaged in different poses make these activities effective at distracting your mind away from your negative thoughts. In addition, these exercises can also help you gain more flexibility, balance, and core strength. However, if you have a debilitating or painful condition that prevents you from doing anything remotely physical, then these activities might not be right for you. However, you can still ask your physician if you can practice these exercises, he might recommend a good physical therapist or gym that can actually help you. Now, if your doctor believes that it is a bad idea for you to do these exercises, heed his words and look elsewhere for a solution.

5. Repetitive Prayers/Chants

This technique is best for those who have relatively short attention spans, so much so that they have trouble focusing on their breath. For this technique, you recite a short prayer, or even a phrase or two from a prayer while focusing on your breath. This method might be more appealing to you if you are religious or if you are a particularly spiritual person.

If you are not religious, or you do not subscribe to any religion, you can do this by replacing the prayers/chants with positive affirmations or lines from your favorite poem.

Psychological experts advise not just choosing one technique out of the list mentioned above. It is much better to try as many of them as you can and then stick to the one/s that you find effective. It is also recommended that you practice these techniques for at least 20 minutes a day for best results, although even just a couple of minutes of practice can help. However, the longer and more often you practice these techniques, the greater the benefits and stress reduction.

Chapter 4.   Anxiety and Its Causes

In order to treat your anxiety, you need to know where it is coming from. Many people describe it as feeling random. It might seem this way because the onset can seem to be out of nowhere. Overthinking causes and contributes to anxiety. They have a relationship to where they both feed off of one another. If you have anxiety, you have a predisposition to overthinking, meanwhile overthinking will increase your levels of anxiety.

There is a reason people who suffer from anxiety disorder are especially prone to overthinking. This is because their mind has become trained to think in worst-case scenarios. For example, they might be driving, and if they feel the bumps that sometimes happen when you're out on the road, and their mind goes to the idea that they hit something. Let me reassure you of something. You would not think you might have hit something or someone. The impact would be like no other. Not everything can be prevented because things happen sometimes, but as long as you are looking at the road ahead of you and do not have any chemicals in your system that could impede your cognitive function, it is unlikely that you are going to get into any serious accident.

Most of the time, it is not random when a person develops anxiety. Sometimes it comes as a delayed reaction of sorts. You might not feel the effects of it while you're going through a stressful situation because your mind is primarily focused on getting through the situation. After the fact, you go through the psychological effects of your situation because you have time to think about it. This is a common thing that happens to people during stressful situations. We stuff our feelings about it because we want to focus on thinking pragmatically and getting ourselves into a better place.

There have been findings that there are certain chemicals in our brain that can cause mood and emotional disorders when off-kilter. However, there also tends to be an environmental component. There are things that can happen to a person that makes them more likely to have difficulty handling stress. That lies where anxiety becomes a disorder. At a certain level, it is natural. When it passes that point and becomes a hindrance in a person's life, it has become a disorder.

Here's essentially how it works. You have an assignment that is due in two weeks. A healthy level of anxiety will make you think, "okay, I need to do this much work in this amount of time. If I want to make the deadline and put out good work, I can't wait around until the last minute. I need to do this much work every day to reach my goals." When it gets to be about the middle of the day, and you haven't done it yet, you start to feel a little uneasy and remind yourself that you need to get going. It's like a person inside you giving you a nudge to get started on your responsibilities because they want to see you succeed. When an anxiety disorder takes over, you will be overcome with fear when you see the requirements and the deadline. You might think, "there's no way I can handle all of this. How will I come up with that much material in such a short amount of time?" Every time you begin to work on it, the blank page intimidates you, and you decide you'd rather spend your time doing something that does not cause you so much stress. Just the thought of working on it makes your heart rate go up. You tell yourself, "I can't handle this today, I'm going to work on it tomorrow when I'm stronger." Then tomorrow comes, and you use the same excuse to put it off.

Any number of things can cause an anxiety disorder. Everyone has times in their lives when their anxiety is at a heightened level. Major life events, such as illness in the family or the loss of a relationship, come with stress naturally. Even good things like getting a new job can cause anxiety.

One of the biggest reasons endings and new beginnings cause anxiety is because then the question becomes, "What comes next?" People have a natural fear of the unknown. Thinking about the new job, you might be confused because you don't know why you aren't jumping for joy. This might be your first job out of school, or it might be a major upgrade from your last one. The working conditions are better, the pay is higher, and your benefits are greater. However, you don't know exactly how this job is going to be. You might have read what will be expected of you in your new role, but that isn't the same as actually being in the job and going through the motions. You haven't met your coworkers yet, and you have only met your boss very briefly. You might have had to move for this job, so that means you're in a whole new environment. You're in a new neighborhood with people you've never met before, and you will have to find where everything is. You're hoping you don't get lost on your first day at work. Is it now becoming more understandable why you'd be nervous about starting a new job?

Sometimes anxiety disorders are born from trauma. When you think of trauma, you probably think of horrible assaults and natural disasters. While these would definitely be a source of anxiety, don't write off your experiences as not being enough to be trauma. If you had a parent who had a short temper and yelled often, and these temper tantrums didn't take much to provoke, it's easy to see where that would leave you with anxiety. You would be unsure of your social interactions. You would interpret everything people do that seems off as a sign that they are about to become angry because you had been exposed to so much anger.

Thinking about the past can bring on anxiety. It can influence your future. Say you did poorly on your most recent exam. If you spend all of your time beating yourself up about it, you will actually be lowering your motivation to do better next time rather than increasing it. Every time you try to study for the next exam, your mind will go back to the last grade, which will distract you from learning new information. Your morale will be low, and that will decrease your self-confidence. People who do not feel good about themselves will not put in their maximum efforts in what they do because they do not feel that they will do well anyways.

There is no undoing the past. Whether your test score was poor because you didn't study as much as you should have, or you studied the wrong material or didn't get enough sleep, or anything else that could've contributed to the failing grade, you can't go back in time and study properly for your previous exam. That is done. Acknowledging what you did wrong in the past should be an aid in doing better in the future, not an instrument to punish yourself.

The fact that you cannot change the past might be discouraging, but try thinking about it in a different way. If we could go back in time and change what we have done, which we can't, we would never be able to start a new beginning because we would be so consumed with fixing what has already happened. Then, what would be the point of improving as a person? You wouldn't have to because you could just turn back time and act differently, which might change the future in ways you wouldn't expect or want.

The permanent state of the past lifts a burden for everyone it places on us. The only thing we need to worry about is the present and how it will affect the future. Let's say you failed that exam because you spent a little too much time playing video games and too little time studying for it. You know what went wrong. Use the errors of the past in that way only. Use them for finding out how you got the undesired outcome so you can prevent getting a similar one later on. This doesn't mean you have a serious problem with gaming or that you need to give it up altogether. It means you need to find a way to incorporate it into your life so that it doesn't impede other aspects of it. Schedule the time you are going to fit into your day that is reserved for gaming and do not let it go past that. Make sure you have done everything you need to do before you start to do the things you want to.

Make a checklist for yourself about what tasks you need to complete before the end of the day. When you find out what material will be on your next exam, begin setting aside a few hours per day to study. If you have homework, get it done before you log into your game accounts. It can be tempting to start indulging in your hobbies when you get home, but there are a few problems with this. If you do wind up getting to your homework or whatever other things you need to do, you will probably wind up putting it off until it's nearly midnight. Once you get it done, it will probably be early in the morning, and then it will take you a little while after that to get to sleep. You will wake up the next morning feeling tired and groggy, and the work you did last night will have been done with a tired mind. Another possibility is that it will be nearly midnight and you'll decide you're too tired to do it tonight, and therefore put it off until tomorrow morning. This causes you to spend the next morning completing your assignment in a blur, and that is if you have enough time to do so and don't have to hand in a paper that has objectives that go uncompleted.

You will actually have more time to indulge in your hobbies and have more fun doing them if you do what you need to do first. If you have the fact that you have some homework you need to do while you are playing your games, the whole experience will be a stressful one because the thought is always hanging over your head- "When am I going to put away the game and get to my assignments? I'll do it right after this match. No, I'm just going to do one more, and then I'll get to it. Okay, I've got 4 hours to it, I've got plenty of time. I still have three hours. I'll play for just a little bit longer. Oh no! I only have half an hour left! Where did the time go? I have to start now! Please let me finish on time."

The very stress of the situation will cause you to stay in your gaming and not tackle your homework. You think, "it's too stressful to think about doing that assignment, and this is relaxing me, so I'm going to keep doing it." However, you're not really relaxed. You can't be because you have a thought looming over you and nagging you in the back of your mind. The stress builds underneath because you know that no amount of doing nothing is going to make that assignment go away. In fact, the more time that passes, the more real it gets because you know you can only put it off for so long.

Keeping a schedule and sticking with it will take a very heavy weight off of your mind. It will also give you a sense of accomplishment. As you check things off your to-do list because you have completed them will make you feel more confident. When the list has been completed, you will feel good about yourself when you go to bed because you will know you have done everything you need to do.

Young adults often feel a great deal of anxiety due to social expectations. The way society is now; you are viewed as a child who needs to ask permission to do anything until you turn 18. At this point, you are seen as an adult in the eyes of the law, and now you are being expected to find out what you are going to do with your life. You've needed to go to your teacher for a bathroom pass, and now you're being bombarded with questions about what you are going to do in the way of a career. You go off to college, where you find out that you need to occupy yourself, and you also are solely responsible for making sure you have all your assignments done on time and know everything you will need to do in the near future. That has not been the case in the past. This is overwhelming. However, at least during your college years, there is a resemblance to your old life. Afterward is when many people find themselves feeling lost.

There is a growing problem following college graduation where people go through a period of not knowing what to do. They are struggling to find a job that is related to the field they got their degree in, or any job at all. This inspires depression, as well as anxiety. In fact, that is why it has earned the name "the post-graduation depression." Graduates feel depressed because they have nothing to do and as a result of the guilt they feel for not having "launched" yet. It is also a time of great fear. You are wondering if you are ever going to be able to start your life. You may be feeling pressure from your parents to get your career started because they are looking at your situation using their own memory of when they were your age, not realizing the economy and society have changed since then, and it is much more difficult for a person to get started with their life now.

First, go to sleep at a reasonable time and get up early in the morning. When you are nervous about your future, you can find yourself in a habit where you fall asleep at a very late hour and then sleep until sometime in the afternoon. This is an avoidance tactic because then you can say, "Well, it's too late to go job hunting now, the day is almost over." You can' avoid your life. It will happen with or without you in the driver's seat. Set a certain number of job applications per day. Eventually, someone will say yes.

Also, think about exploring alternative career paths. For example, if you excel in writing, or just have an interest in it, you might want to consider freelance writing. You might choose to supplement your income with it, and for some people, it is their full-time career. It might seem impossible to start, but once you get that first client, you've gotten a foot in. Then you will find your second client. Most companies need a writer. You can be a blogger, a technical writer, a fictional writer, anything you can possibly think of; there is a niche for it in the writing business.

While you are searching for your career, do not beat yourself up about where you are compared to everyone else. You are where you are, and that is fine. Before you get started, use the time you have in between for self-discovery. Once you get into the workforce, it will be a consistent thing, so use this time in between for self-betterment. Figure out who you are, and not just in terms of finding your career. In fact, when you have done some self-reflection, it might be easier to find what you want to do with your life. Feel free to try a few career paths before you settle on one. Think long and hard about whether this is something you could see yourself doing long-term. Do not beat yourself up about what you haven't done. That won't get you anywhere. Celebrate what you have done, and know that you are going to do more in the future.

Holding wasted time against you is pointless and will only lead to wasting more time. It is a road to nowhere. Making yourself suffer over a mistake does not undo it. Treat yourself the way you would a close friend who had made a mistake. You would not remind them over and over of the things they did wrong, and if someone tried to do that, you would probably stand up for them and tell that person they couldn't talk to your friend that way. Be a friend to yourself. Stand up for yourself and tell that voice in your mind it doesn't get to insult you, and you take it lying down. Let it know you will make up your own mind about yourself and that your self-esteem will have nothing to do with any unkind remarks it makes.

The most important thing to remember is that once you have improved your behavior, you need to congratulate yourself on that instead of focusing on the errors of the past. Not only will you not undo those mistakes, but you will prevent yourself from achieving future successes. Absolve yourself of the past so your focus can be on the future.

Chapter 5.   Dealing with procrastination

Is there really a connection between overthinking and procrastination? Why yes, there is, and it is actually more harmful than your garden-variety procrastination. Procrastination as a result of overthinking is called "analysis paralysis", this means you have so many thoughts running through your mind at once that you cannot pick just one. You have to pick apart every option that you have until you are satisfied, which rarely is the case (overthinkers usually never come to a conclusive choice).

This is one of the ugliest facets of overthinking that does not really get too much attention, mainly because people do not equate procrastination with overthinking and anxiety; they believe that procrastination is just a byproduct of laziness, and that is sadly not the case.

What is Analysis Paralysis?

Before going deeper into this harmful habit, consider the ancient fable about the Fox and the Cat. The Fox and the Cat were talking in the forest, the Fox said "I can never be caught by the hunters because I have hundreds of ideas on how I can easily escape them!" The cat, who is a bit jealous, said "You are so lucky, I only know one way to escape capture." Upon hearing this, the fox just gloated and chided the cat for not being as smart as he is.

Suddenly, in the distance, the pair heard the bawling of a group of hunting hounds. The cat quickly clambered up the tallest tree he could find so he can escape. The fox, on the other hand, just stood there contemplating which of his hundred or so escape ideas he should use today; he got so engrossed in his thoughts that the hunters' hounds caught up to him and captured the bewildered Fox. Originally, the lesson of the story is to not let your hubris cloud your judgment, but it can also be used as a classic example of the dangers of Analysis Paralysis.

Analysis paralysis, as the name suggests, is the state of over-analyzing (or overthinking) situations so much that a clear decision or action is not taken, which leads to the paralysis of the outcome.

When a person is experiencing analysis paralysis, he gets so engrossed into the analyzing and evaluating of data need to make a correct decision, just like the fox in the fable, you will never reach the right choice, you will just be stuck there with your mouth agape and unable to take any form of action.

Analysis paralysis happens when one's fear of what could potentially go wrong is stronger than the actual realistic potential for success. This imbalance results in the suppression of a person's decision-making in an effort to preserve and try out other existing options. This surplus of available options can make the situation more overwhelming than it actually is and thus causing a sort of mental paralysis, which renders the person unable to make up his mind.

Analysis paralysis becomes an even bigger problem when a decision is direly needed in critical situations, but the person in charge cannot decide fast enough, thus resulting in an even bigger problem than before if only a fast decision was made.

Casual Analysis Paralysis

There are different forms of analysis paralysis, but there are two main distinctions: personal and conversational analysis paralysis.

Personal Analysis

Casual analysis paralysis can happen when you are trying to make a personal decision, but you cannot because you are overanalyzing the situation that you are currently facing. This happens when the sheer volume of information that you have to process starts to become too overbearing. You get so burdened by the amount of things in your head that you cannot, for the life of you, make a rational decision.

There are some cases wherein the decision-maker could successfully analyze every possible outcome, and even write them all down, but then inexplicably trash all of them because he did not like how he analyzed them. Not only is this a waste of mental and physical energy, it is also a waste of your time, which is not a good look when this often happens to you while you are at work.

Conversational Analysis

Analysis paralysis can happen at any time during any typical conversation, however, conversational analysis paralysis usually happens when discussing intellectual and heavy topics. During the course of an intellectual discussion, a person might over-analyze a specific issue, up to the point that the original subject of the conversation is lost. This usually happens because complex intellectual subjects are interconnected with other intellectual issues, and the pursuit of these other branches of discussion somehow makes logical sense to the participants. However, this actually does not make much sense because it muddles the conversation, and the topic of discussion strays so far from the original.

How Overthinking is Holding You Back

Delaying action while over-analyzing available information does not help with productivity. A 2010 survey done by LexisNexis (a legal research company) showed that employees spend more than half of their workday just receiving and analyzing information rather than doing their jobs. However, that is just what people see on the surface. Studies in the field of psychology and neuroscience showed that analysis paralysis takes a bigger toll on you than just wasting your time.

Here are some of the ways that analysis paralysis is holding you back:

1. Analysis paralysis negatively affects your performance on mentally-demanding tasks

Your working memory allows you to focus only on the information that you need to finish your tasks. Unfortunately, you only have a limited supply of working memory per day. Once you have used up all of your available working memory you cannot fit any more information in your brain.

Research showed that high-stress situations can lead to decreased performance when doing mentally-demanding tasks, these are the tasks that where you rely heavily on your working memory to finish. In addition, if there are more participants who want to perform well on a task, the more their performance suffers. Researchers believe that anxiety and stress produces distracting thoughts that take up a lot of your working memory that you could have used to work on your tasks.

2. Analysis paralysis eats at your willpower

A study published by the National Academy of Science looked at the decisions made by parole board judges within a 10-month period. The study found the judges were more likely to grant prisoners parole early in the morning and immediately after eating lunch. They were also more likely to deny parole when the cases are placed on their desk after the end of a particularly long work session. This phenomenon held true over the course of the study, a span that encompassed more than 1,100 cases, regardless of the severity of the crime, which makes it more than just a simple coincidence.

What could have explained these rather surprising, and disturbing discoveries? The judges suffered from what psychology professionals call "decision fatigue". Every decision that people make during the course of the day, like whether to hit the snooze button or not, having fish or chicken for lunch, and other times when you have to choose between several options, they all draw from a limited reserve of willpower. Imagine your willpower as if it was a muscle; the more you use it, the faster you wear it out, which then leaves you mentally exhausted and feeling overwhelmed. This is why dieters have no problem keeping up with their program when it is still early in the day and they are still relatively full after eating a healthy breakfast and lunch, but they are more likely to succumb to the temptation of eating junk food during their afternoon coffee break. During the course of the day the amount of willpower you will have left will dwindle, but it will replenish itself in the morning, only for you to repeat the cycle all over again.

The things that you do without thinking, like brushing your teeth, or putting on your clothes, take little to no willpower at all, so you can still somehow get through the day. However, when you take too long at making a decision, you are quickly depleting what little amount of willpower you have left in your mind.

When you are running low on willpower, your capability to make wise decisions are affected. This means you are more likely to choose to eat unhealthy food, skip exercising, and procrastinate working on your side projects. In short, when you over-analyze your decisions, making more difficult choices even harder in the long run.

3. When you overthink you become less happy

Back in 1956, Herman Simon, an economist, first coined the term "satisficer", which is basically a decision-making style that gives more weight to solutions that are just adequate rather than those that are optimal. Satisficers are people who will only decide once most, if not all of their criteria are met. For instance, they will only stay in a hotel if the in-house restaurant serves the kind of pasta that he wants.

In comparison, "maximizers" want to make the best possible decision. Even when they see something that meets their criteria, they will not make a decision until they have compared it with other possible options. They will waste a lot of their time and energy to find options, regardless if they have little or no significance to the actual task.

Regardless if you are a satisficer or a maximizer, research suggests that your behavior has a huge negative impact on your well-being. These studies found that:

Maximizers are significantly less satisfied, happy, optimistic, has less self-esteem, and has significantly more regrets compared to satisficers.

Maximizers are more prone to suffering from buyer's regret. They cannot help but compare themselves to others and engaging in counterfactual thinking. For instance, they immediately feel sad when they buy an item, they almost immediately think what would have happened if they chose the other item instead. Instead of happiness when they made a purchase, they just feel regret.

Maximizers are more likely to fall into a negative mood once they notice that they did not perform as well as their peers. It's like professional jealousy, but it also spills over to the person's personal life. They constantly compare themselves to people they know, and if they do not perceive themselves to be better than their peers, it will be reason enough to worry oneself into analysis paralysis.

Although analyzing every option available does lead to the absolute best outcome, maximizing will only lead to more stress, anxiety, regret, and you will still not be entirely happy when you do make a decision.

Okay, so now you know how overthinking any decision can and will only make you anxious, kills your productivity, and overall lowers your self-esteem, but what can you do to stop it?

Here are some simple ways that can help you stop over-analyzing your options, avoid getting trapped by analysis paralysis, and just start doing all the things that you are supposed to do:

Structure your day according to the decisions that are most important to you

Not all decisions are equal. For instance, deciding on a brand of toothpaste to buy later is less worthy of your limited supply of willpower compared to, say deciding on whether to agree to the terms of your suppliers or not.

Your ability to make quality decisions wane deteriorate with every choice you make throughout the day, regardless if said decisions are inconsequential or not. This is why you need to schedule your day so that you can minimize the number of decisions that you need to make every day. For instance, divide your workload so that you tackle your most important tasks first thing in the morning, while you still have a lot of willpower to spare. In addition, automate your small, insignificant decisions so that you do not have to waste energy on them. Take Mark Zuckerberg for instance, as head of the biggest social media network in the world, he cannot be bothered to waste energy deciding what clothes he needs to wear, so he wears the same grey t-shirt and jeans combo every day of the week, unless the occasion needs him to change.

Do not even try to tackle big decisions late in the afternoon, you will only drain whatever amount of willpower you have left in your body, and it will only make you feel overwhelmed, cranky, and regretful. If you find yourself getting caught in a downward spiral of overthinking and analysis paralysis, wrestle yourself out of it by doing something that is completely unrelated to your previous task; or better yet, call it a day. Just come back to the task the next morning when your willpower reserves are refilled.

Limit the amount of information you consume

There is a virtually limitless amount of information that you can consult for any sort of problem that you face. For instance, when you are writing a book report, you have an endless number of websites that you can go to for all the important information that you need to know. This is why you need to approach your research with solid intention.

Sherlock Holmes, the greatest literary detective to ever grace the pages of a book, is infamous for only consuming information that he could use in his profession. For instance, Holmes has little to no knowledge about Literature, Philosophy, and Politics, which are subjects that he deems unimportant to his profession. However, his skills in Botany, Human Anatomy, and Geology are variable, he only took various tidbits from the subjects to help him in his cases; for instance, regarding botany, Holmes has an extensive library of knowledge about poisonous plants, especially the ones from the belladonna family.

Holmes knows that the capacity of his brain is very limited so he only stores the information that he needs. Be like Sherlock Holmes, for your workday, only consume information that you will need to finish your tasks; turn off your smartphone, do not open your social media accounts, and do not open your personal email, do those things at the end of the day.

Set a deadline for yourself to make yourself accountable

According to Parkinson's Law, your work will expand to fill the space of time that you set aside for it. For instance, give yourself an hour to finish a task, and you will see that it will take exactly an hour. Give yourself 15 minutes to finish the same task and you could finish it within fifteen minutes. The same holds for decision-making; if you set a deadline for a decision, it will force you to make an efficient decision within that set amount of time.

However, tricking yourself to commit to a self-imposed deadline can be quite hard, but you should find a way that you can hold yourself accountable. One way to do this is to make your deadline as public as possible. Tell a co-worker that you gave yourself a deadline to finish your tasks, or better yet, announce in your social media accounts that you are giving yourself a deadline. The more people who know about your deadline, the better.

4. Stick to your main objective

Identifying your main objective and then sticking to it can help you overcome your tendency to fall into analysis paralysis.

All of your decisions should center around your main objective. If a decision does not affect your main objective in any way, set it aside for later. Only think about the things that you need to do to get closer to your main objective. Because you know your main objective, it helps you make quick and decisive choices because you can immediately assess the options available to you.

Talk with someone else so you can escape your own mind

People are naturally predisposed to overestimate just how unhappy they will be when something bad happens to them, and also overestimate just how happy they will be when things go their way. Studies have shown that complete strangers are actually better at predicting your own satisfaction or dissatisfaction from a decision that you yourself made.

Whenever you are bogged down by a decision that you have to make, just asking another person for his or her opinions about the subject will help you make a decision that you are actually okay with, as compared to making the decision yourself without other people's input.

The next time you find yourself overthinking over a singular important issue, ask a co-worker if you could bother him or her for a minute or so, or you can consult with your supervisor, or if you have one, your mentor. When you present your deliberations to other people, you are actually forcing yourself to synthesize the information in a more clear and concise manner (compared to how muddled and messy the information was when it was still in your mind).

In addition, having someone else validate your ideas, especially if that someone is a person whom you respect, might just be the thing that you need to get over your self-doubt and gain enough confidence to take further action.

Chapter 6.   How to Stop Overthinking

Overthinking is one of the most common mental conditions in the world, and unfortunately, it is also one of the most debilitating. You might think that it is no big deal, everybody gets lost in their thoughts sometimes, right? But when overthinking hits, you, it hits you hard. This is especially troubling if you have trouble with anxiety.

Now, if you have any previous experience in falling into the almost endless spiraling pit of despair that is overthinking, then you know just how horrible it is. Overthinking can prevent you from enjoying the things that you used to love doing, like going to parties, walking in the park, or just meeting with friends. Overthinking can also negatively affect your performance at work, it makes you lose motivation, makes you procrastinate on your tasks, and thus ruining whatever chances of job progression you might have. Overthinking can also ruin your personal relationships; no one wants to be around a person who is always complaining, cranky, and has such a short temper, so you will have very few friends, and they might not be sticking around for much longer.

If the picture painted above seems familiar to you, then you are probably already aware that there is something wrong about you, and that you are already desperate to find a way to fix yourself and start living again. However, it seems like everything you do seems futile, it's as if there is always an insurmountable hurdle in front of you. Overthinking not only leaves you mentally drained, but it also makes you feel exhausted physically. It's like having an energy vampire latched permanently on your neck, and it is constantly feeding on what little mental and physical energy you have.

However, you should not lose hope just yet; there are plenty of ways that you can use to overcome your chronic overthinking problem. But first, you need to start with understanding the core problem; you need to know what overthinking is, and from there, you can start looking for the most viable solutions.

Overthinking Disorder Defined:

Everyone gets sucked into the rabbit hole of obsessive thoughts sometimes, and when it happens occasionally, then it is fine. However, when overthinking starts to consume your life, that is when it becomes a chronic mental problem.

Not everyone is prone to overthink, but some are more likely to suffer from it. For instance, people with a history of struggling with anxiety are almost always dealing with overthinking and its consequences daily. In fact, overthinking is actually one of the triggers that cause anxiety in most people.

Even if you do not have any history of mental health problems, if you consider yourself as a "problem solver" of sorts, then you are prone to overthinking. The thing you consider as your most valuable asset, which is your analytical mind, can become your worst enemy when your overthinking is triggered. Analytical thinkers are the ones that are easily pulled into an endless loop of unproductive and irrational thoughts.

In addition, if you are at a low point in your life where you have unusually high levels of uncertainty, it can trigger your overthinking disorder. If you just experienced a major loss in your life, like you just got fired from your job, your significant other left you, or someone close to you recently died, these events might cause your mind to an uncontrollable spiral of unproductive thoughts.

What are the Symptoms of Overthinking?:

Now that you have an idea of what overthinking is, the next thing that you need to know is the signs of overthinking to look out for. Knowing the symptoms will inform you that you might need to be wary of the status of your mental health, maybe consider getting professional help. You can somehow gauge how deep into overthinking you are by identifying which symptoms have already manifested; if you find that you have signs of being a chronic overthinker, then you should probably consider getting professional help ASAP.

You Have Trouble Getting to Sleep?:

You cannot turn off your thoughts, even when you try; in fact, your thoughts actually start racing even faster when you try to stop them. All of these worries and doubts swirling in your head agitates you and prevents you from getting enough rest.

Overthinkers know the feeling of not getting enough sleep, almost too well actually. Insomnia happens because you have no control over your brain; you cannot shut off the chain of negative thoughts going through your mind at a hundred miles an hour. All of the things that worried you throughout the day come back just when you hit the sack, and you feel so wired that you cannot fall asleep.

If you are having difficulty calming your mind on your own, you can try different relaxing activities before you go to bed. There are plenty of things that might help you ease your mind just enough to let you get some sleep, like meditation, writing on a journal, adult coloring books, drawing, painting, reading a book, or even just having a nice conversation with a loved one. Do anything that can shift your attention away from the negative thoughts long enough for you to get some sleep.

You Start to Self-Medicate?:

Numerous medical researches have discovered that most people suffering from overthinking disorder have turned to use recreational drugs, alcohol, overeating, or other ways to get a grip on their emotions somehow. Overthinkers feel the need to rely on external stimuli because they believe that their internal resources (aka their minds) are already compromised.

It is never a good idea to turn to try to treat yourself from overthinking. Odds are, you will still be overthinking afterward, and you have to deal with a different problem brought about by your self-medication.

You are Always Tired?:

If you are constantly feeling tired, you need to take action. Fatigue is your body's way of telling you to listen to it because there is something wrong going on; you should not ignore it and just hop from one activity to the next.

Usually, fatigue is caused by physical overexertion and lack of rest. However, overthinking can also cause fatigue and exhaustion. Your mind is like a muscle; if you are constantly burdening it with dozens of heavy, negative thoughts all the time, and not even giving it some time to recover, it will get exhausted and cause you to burn out.

Back when humans were still living off the land, people did not have that many things to worry about, which means they do not have quite as many things to think about as well. In today's modern world, people lead complicated lives that require them to accomplish a lot of things in a short amount of time. In this fast-paced world, the need to slow down every once in a while is crucial for people's well-being. So, whenever you feel fatigued, or better yet, if you feel close to it, slow things down and figure out what your body and your mind need before doing anything else.

You Tend to Overanalyze Everything?:

Overthinkers have one major problem, and that is that they always feel that they need to be in control of everything. They plan out every aspect of their lives, some of them even go as far as planning up to the smallest detail. They feel that doing this is the only way they can feel safe, but it always seems to backfire at them because it is actually impossible to plan for everything that will happen in their lives.

Even so, they still continue to plan out their futures, and they get anxious when unexpected things happen, and they always seem to be unexpected things happening all the time. Overthinkers hate dealing with things that they do not have control over, and they fear the unknown. When unexpected problems do surface, they cause them to sit and mull things over instead of taking immediate action to solve the unexpected problem. Numerous medical studies have shown that overthinking leads to making poor judgment calls, which is why overthinking does not really help.

When you catch yourself just before you start overthinking, try your best to bring your thoughts back to the present by taking deep breaths and thinking happy thoughts. Before your negative thoughts go rampant inside your head, acknowledge them, and think about what they can do for you presently; doing this alone is usually enough to get rid of these negative thoughts because you will discover that their only purpose is to cause you stress.

You are Afraid of Failure?:

You fancy yourself a perfectionist, and you often think about how awful you would feel if you were to fail somehow. This fear of failure can be so strong that it paralyzes you, and it keeps you from learning from your prior mistakes, which often lead to you repeating them.

Overthinkers often cannot accept failure, and they will do everything they can to avoid it. Ironically, they think that the only way to not fail is to do nothing at all. They mistakenly believe that to avoid failure, they should not put themselves in a position to fail at all, which also means they are not in the position to succeed as well.

If this sounds like you, remember that you are more than just your failures; no one could even remember the last time that you screwed up, it's just you. Also, keep in mind that it is impossible to escape failure, and you should never avoid it at all. For failure allows you to grow and evolve.

You are Afraid of What the Future Holds?:
Instead of being excited about the things that you are yet to experience, your anxiety and fear of what could go wrong paralyze you into doing nothing.

If you are afraid of what the future could bring, then your fear keeps you trapped inside your own mind. Research shows that this fear of the future can be so crippling that sufferers tend to turn to drugs and/or alcohol just so they can tune out the negative thoughts that are clamoring inside their heads.

You Don't Trust Your Own Judgment?:
You cannot help yourself from second-guessing all of your decisions, from your outfit, what you will be having for lunch, or even what you will be doing for the day. You are always afraid that you will be making the wrong

choices, and you often rely on others to reassure you that you made the right call.

Overthinkers, as mentioned earlier, are natural *perfectionists*; they constantly analyze, re-analyze, and re-analyze again, all situations that they find themselves in. They do not want to put themselves in a position where there is even a slight chance of failure. They do not want to make the wrong choice, so they take their sweet time making up their minds; they do not trust themselves enough to make the right decision for anything. They are

so out of touch from their intuition that all of their decisions come from their brain, and this is not always right as there are times when you just need to follow your gut instinct. Also, if your brain is bogged down from dozens of negative thoughts, it is hard to make a clear decision.

You Suffer from Frequent Tension Headaches?
Tension headaches feel as if there is a thick rubber band wrapped around your temples, and it is slowly getting tighter. Aside from the headache, you might also feel a sharp pain or stiffness in your neck. If you suffer from chronic tension headaches, it is a sign that you are overworking yourself, and you need a rest.

And by rest, it also includes rest from mental activities, like overthinking. Headaches are a sign that your body needs to take a break. This includes your mind. Besides, you might not notice it, but when you overthink, you are actually thinking of the same things over and over again.

Overthinkers usually have negative thought patterns that loop around themselves. To fight this, you need to break this loop by reinforcing positive thoughts. Take deep breaths, and focus your mind on every time your chest rises and falls, being mindful of the present will help you get rid of negative thoughts and the tension headache that came with them.

Stiff Joints and Muscle Pain:

It might sound far-fetched, but overthinking can actually affect your entire body, not just your mind. And once your physical body is affected by your out of control negative thoughts, it will not be long until your emotional well-being gets hit too. Until you address and get rid of the underlying issues that cause you to overthink, the body pains will continue. Overthinking might start in your mind, but its effects will gradually creep into the other parts of your body.

You Cannot Stay In the Present?:

When you overthink, you will find it difficult living in the present moment and actually enjoy your life as it happens. Overthinking causes you to lose focus on the things happening around you, you are so engrossed at thinking about your problems over and over that it seems like you are trapped inside your own mind. If your mind gets bogged down by a ton of unnecessary thoughts, you are removing yourself from the present, and this can and will negatively affect your personal relationships.

You need to open yourself to the world around you; do not let yourself get too wrapped up in negative thoughts. The only thoughts that you should allow inside your mind are those that serve your well-being, ignore, and forget about the ones that bring you down. There is so much beauty in life, and the opportunities for incredible experiences are unlimited. However, you can only appreciate them if you can manage to tune out the idle chatter in your mind and start listening to your heart instead.

Different Causes of Overthinking:

Again, there is nothing wrong about thinking about your problems so you can think of a solution for them, it becomes worrisome when you have a bad habit of twisting narratives around in your head until you can see every angle and side to it. Overthinking is not productive as it just makes you dwell over your problems; you are not looking for a solution for them, and you are only making yourself feel miserable.

To find an effective way to break your overthinking habit, you need to find out what caused it in the first place. Below are some of the more common reasons as to why people tend to overthink their problems rather than actually find a solution for them.

1. Lack of Self-confidence

If you are not self-confident, you tend to doubt every little thing that you say or do. When you hesitate, even a little, about the things that you want to do, you are letting uncertainty and fear creep into your mind, and it will be very difficult to get them out of there. You can never really tell what your decisions will take you; even if you planned every little detail, the outcome will still not be exactly what you hoped for (it could either be better or worse than what you planned). This is why you should learn to take risks and not torture yourself when you did not get the results you wished for.

2. When You Worry Too Much

It is only natural to worry when you encounter new and unfamiliar things and events. However, if you worry too much that you cannot even imagine a positive outcome, then it will trigger you to overthink. This is problematic because worry attracts even more problems, sometimes it creates ones out of thin air, which causes overthinking to go even deeper. Instead of mulling over how things could go wrong, it is better to entertain more positive thoughts, like how much better you would feel if a certain even turns in your favor.

3. When You Overthink to Protect Yourself

Some people believe that they can protect themselves from troubles whenever they overthink, but the truth is that overthinking is a trap that kills your progress. Overthinking and not doing anything to change the status quo might seem good, but stifling your progress is never a good thing at all. Also, when you overthink, you are not really staying in the same position. You are actually undoing whatever amount of progress you achieved thus far.

4. You are unable to "Turn Off" Your Mind

Many overthinkers became that way because they cannot seem to get their minds off their problems no matter how hard they try. People who are sensitive to stress live as if they are constantly wound up tightly; they have somehow forgotten how to relax and change their chain of thoughts. Overthinking happens when a person stresses too much on a single problem, and he could not turn his focus away from it.

5. You are Always Chasing After Perfection

Being a perfectionist is not necessarily a good thing. In fact, one could argue that being a perfectionist is not good at all. Most people who struggle with perfectionism are constantly anxious. They often wake up in the middle of the night, thinking of the things that they could have done better. Being a perfectionist causes overthinking because you are always trying to outdo yourself.

Chapter 7.   How to Stop Overthinking with Mindfulness Meditation

You're familiar with meditation, but what you're going to learn here is how to overcome your excessive thoughts is *mindfulness meditation.* This form of meditation encourages us to remain aware and present by focusing on nothing except awareness of your existing surroundings. Meditation is actually an ancient technique that trains the brain to strengthen its powers of concentration. Sort of like a gym workout, except for your brain this time. Some *archeologists* believe that meditation could be as old as 5,000 years, although scientists only really began studying the brains of those who meditated regularly approximately 60 or so years ago. Still, the fact that this practice has managed to survive for this long means there's something extraordinarily powerful and effective about it.

What researchers have discovered throughout their studies is that meditation changes the structure of your brain, thereby making it a lot more powerful. Long-term meditators have been known to develop almost superhuman-like abilities. For example, their ability to stay calm even in the most stressful situations that would have non-meditators at their wit's end. They could also produce more creative and original ideas, not to mention the better memory they had compared to those who didn't meditate regularly. One *experiment* revealed how meditating monks were able to dry icy wet sheets in cold temperatures by raising and controlling *their body temperature* through the power of meditation.

To understand the way meditation affects us, we need to look at the recent discoveries about how the human brain operates. In the last 10 years alone, what scientists have come to discover is that each time we learn, feel or think something, a new connection appears in the brain. What we repeat the most, like habits, make these connections increase in strength. Simultaneously, the connections that we don't use grow weaker over time until they finally disappear from the mind altogether. This is why habits are automatic and require very little thought to carry them out. For instance, the way you practice brushing your teeth each day makes the task seem a lot more effortless than trying something new like going for a jog in the morning before work. However, if you were to stop brushing your teeth for a few days, surprisingly, it will begin to feel like it requires slightly more effort to execute than it did before.

Some *researchers* have gone so far as to suggest that we don't choose our behavior. Instead, our behavior is programmed by the neural connections in the brain. The brain is like an iceberg, where the tip of the iceberg (the smallest part) represents the conscious mind. Here are all the things we *can choose* consciously, like eating or solving a complicated math problem. The larger part of the iceberg, the one that is submerged and hidden below the surface, is where the unconscious mind resides. The unconscious mind is the one responsible for most of our behaviors since this also happens to be where our thoughts and feelings reside. The unconscious mind, therefore, causes behavior like reacting to arguments in the same way or reacting emotionally more than once, even when we know it's the wrong approach to take. This happens because we're not aware that we're being controlled by the unconscious part of the brain.

The neural connections in the unconscious part of the mind are strong. This leads to a lot of people to believe that they "cannot change" the way they react or act in certain situations. This automatic response is what we call *personality,* but in actual fact, they are the unconscious mind, emotions, and habits that we keep repeating because it's all we know how to do.

Research has found out that mindfulness meditation can improve focus, memory as well as reduce fixation on negative emotions and lessen impulsive, emotional reactions. *This can be changed*. Everything we know and learn can always be developed through practice. You can train your brain to do what you want it to. To initiate the changes you want to see, you need to first change your brain by creating new connections and then practicing these connections until they become strong enough to be automatic. The things that you find hard to do now will become easier with practice.

Think about how you struggled to exercise in the beginning. Or even when you were a child learning how to read. Those first few attempts felt like an immense struggle back then, but since you kept practicing and persisting, the behavior became automatic. Now, you can quickly breeze through a sentence with ease, and it doesn't take much persuasion for you to put on your workout clothes and start working up a sweat. This is where the meditation practice comes in. It helps us change the structure of the brain by creating new connections in several areas of the brain.

Overthinking leads to continuous stress, and continuous stress leads to mental health issues. Depression and anxiety are very clear examples of what can happen to you if you continue to let your thoughts be the one in control. Meditation decreases the size of the amygdala; the brains fear center, and where all our negative thoughts and emotions come from. Meditation also decreases the levels of cortisol, which leads to an enhanced ability to deal with stressful situations a lot better. During meditation, you'll learn the very crucial skill of learning *how to watch your thoughts and emotions* without reacting to them, which is required for mindfulness. With frequent meditation, there's a possibility of significantly changing your behavior and personality.

How to Meditate

Meditation is one of the simplest forms of mental training you can do. All that is needed is for you to concentrate on your breathing as you allow your thoughts and feelings to come and go. With continuous practice, your skills of concentration, awareness, and attention significantly increase. It does sound easy (and it will be with practice), but in the beginning, you might find that concentrating on your breath is not as easy as it sounds after all.

Where Should I Meditate?

Technically, meditation can be done anywhere you like since it is an exercise for the mind. You could meditate while sitting in a chair or on the floor, even while you're lying down in bed. However, it is recommended that you avoid meditating in bed where possible since you might fall asleep and find it difficult to concentrate.

Sitting down on the floor with your back and spine straight is considered the *optimal* and beneficial way to meditate. This position keeps you wide awake and allows you to sit for a prolonged period while you carry out your concentration session.

What Do I Do When I Meditate?

What should you do with your body while you meditate? Well, the first thing to do is to be aware of the way your feet are positioned. Many regular and seasoned meditators will advise that your feet should be on top of each other. This is not always necessary, though, and you don't have to do it if it doesn't feel comfortable. Beginners might prefer to have their feet crisscrossed on top of each other, sort of like a pretzel while your arms are resting on your thighs. Your hands should be resting on top of each other and form the shape of a cup. If you want to touch your thumbs together while you do this, it's perfectly okay. What matters is that your arms feel relaxed as you keep your back straight and your head level.

Your head should not be tilted upwards or downwards. Relax and look forward naturally. As for your eyes, you have the option of meditating with them open or closed, depending on your preference. Most seasoned meditators prefer to do it with their eyes closed for greater concentration, but again do what feels comfortable and what works for you. If you do choose to meditate with your eyes open, avoid focusing on an object in front of you. Instead, try to look into the distance.

How Long Do I Need to Meditate?

As a beginner, you'll want to set an alarm before you begin your meditation session. When you first start meditating, time tends to feel a lot slower because your body and mind are trying to get used to this new habit. By setting an alarm, you eliminate the constant need to wonder how much time you have left or how long you've been doing it already. Beginners can aim to set about 5-minutes on the clock to start with as you acclimatize yourself to this practice. Once meditation becomes a daily practice and you get used to sitting in this position, you can gradually increase your time blocks, meditating for as long as you want. The recommended time for meditation is approximately 10 to 20 minutes a day.

What Do I Do While I Meditate?

This is the tricky part. There are several forms of meditation that can be carried out. Certain forms of meditation encourage you to focus on your breathing (mindfulness) and loving-kindness, while others may involve chanting a mantra (affirmation). Mindfulness breathing meditation is one of the most commonly taught forms of meditation, and given that you're trying to overcome your overthinking habit, this is the meditation you want to start with.

Mindfulness meditation is easy to learn, and it is considered just as insightful and powerful as any other form. With this form of meditation, you want to start by making sure that you're breathing through your nose. Once you've established a rhythm, focus *all your attention* on your breath and observe the way the air flows in and out of your body. Pay attention to the air flowing in and out of your nostrils; observe the way your breath makes the transition from inhale to exhale. Even pay attention to the little pauses that happen between the moment you inhale and exhale. Don't judge. Don't criticize. Just stay calm and observe; that's all you need to do.

You'll quickly notice that thoughts begin to appear in your mind and will try to distract you from this simple task you're supposed to be concentrating on. If you notice your mind wandering, don't worry. Simply pull your thoughts back toward your breathing and focus on your breath. This is how you start training your mindfulness muscle. Many beginners often find it extremely hard to focus on nothing but the breath, so you're not alone if you feel this is a struggle. If this happens, don't be too hard on yourself or too critical, this is perfectly normal. All you need to do is bring your attention right back to your breathing whenever the mind wanders.

How Often Should I Do It?

Ideally, you want to aim to make mindfulness meditation a daily habit. The more you do it, the easier it will become to focus on nothing but your breath as your mindfulness muscle grows stronger. Meditating every day gives you the best chance of seeing the benefits quickly. You could do it once a day, twice a day, or even three times a day if you have the time. You can do it as many times a day as you like, but what matters most is that you do it EVERY DAY.

How Soon Can I Expect to See the Benefits?

Well, you need to be doing it every day to see the benefits a lot sooner. The length of time you spend meditating daily will also play a factor in how quickly you start experiencing the benefits. Ultimately, it is difficult to fix an exact time frame since the experience is going to differ from one person to the next. Some people happen to be less mindful in general because of the lifestyle they lead and the way they grew up, so they might need more time before they begin seeing any real change. The best thing you can do is to just keep practicing and don't compare your journey to someone else's. It doesn't matter how fast or slow the benefits start to happen. What matters is that if you keep at it, *they will happen.*

Why You Need to Practice Mindfulness

Overthinking is a distraction, and that is just one of the many reasons why you need mindfulness to live in the present. As painful as some of the difficult parts of life is, that's what *living* is, and we need to embrace it wholeheartedly, both good and bad. Mindfulness teaches us that it is still possible to find happiness even in the darkest times. It's not always possible to be mindful 100% of the time, but the following reasons will remind you why you need to make an effort to live mindfully every day:

- *It's the* **Only Real Time** *to Live Properly* - We spend more time than we should when we continue living in our heads worrying about the past or the future. We worry about what we cannot change and what we have no control over. Mindfulness is the only tool that is effective enough to get you to break the habit bit by bit. The past only exists in our memory, and the future is yet to come. This means that the only *real living* that takes place is your present. The here and now.

- *Your Thoughts Are Less Likely to Sweep You Away* - It's impossible to get carried away when you know exactly what's going on with your thoughts, emotions, and feelings. Instead of getting swept away by your excessive thoughts this time, mindfulness will turn you into an observer. Think of your thoughts like a flowing river. You cannot forcefully stop the water from flowing. When you enter the river, you will get swept away, so instead, the better thing to do would be to practice sitting by the river, watching it flow by. By becoming an observer, your thoughts and emotions loosen the hold they have over you. You no longer feel powerless, and like you're drowning. You become calm, composed, and this time you're the one in control. Like the flowing river, the thoughts won't stay forever unless you choose to let them. You're not trying to fight your thoughts, judge it or forcefully change it. You're just there to observe.

- *It Builds Stronger Relationships* - Among the more common worrying thoughts that tend to plague the mind of an overthinker is the anxiety they feel about what others think of them. It's hard to form great connections when you're not really *listening* to what is being said to you. Sure, you're there in front of the speaker, but when you're preoccupied with your thoughts, you're not actively listening, and you miss out on important information that could have been used to strengthen your relationship. Mindfulness can change the type of conversations you have with people by encouraging you to pay attention and be open to their needs. To put aside everything else for those few minutes and pay attention to what is being said to you. Once you start actively listening, conversations seem richer and more meaningful. The other person begins to engage more when they notice you're actively paying attention to them too. It makes them feel like what they have to say matters, and that, in turn, encourages them to be more open and share more of their life with you.

- *It Makes You Aware You Have Everything You Need to Be Happy -* We keep searching for happiness and then getting frustrated when it's seemingly hard to attain. Through mindfulness, however, you realize you already have everything you need to be happy. You couldn't see it because you were too distracted by your thoughts. When you start living in the present, the realization begins to dawn on you that there is no real need to hold on to the things that make you unhappy. You don't need to hold on to grievances about your past or worry about your future. Your eyes begin to open to the fact that perhaps a lot of the problems you have today were created in your mind, and if you break those problems down bit by bit, there might not be anything much to worry about after all. Feeling grateful for the life you have is your biggest defense against negativity. You don't need to rely on external or material things to make you happy when you feel good from within.
- *It Reminds You to Take Care of Yourself -* You can't take care of anyone else if you're not taking care of yourself first. Self-care can be a tough lesson for overthinkers since they tend to cross their boundaries. Their excessive thinking could lead them to push too hard until they eventually get burned out. Mindfulness makes you more aware of your strengths and your boundaries. You're less likely to push yourself too far when you're aware of the way that your mind

and your body feel. You begin respecting your body more, and you slowly lose the urge to keep up with society's fast-paced expectations if it is going to make you unhappy doing it. It's perfectly okay to do what makes you happy without having to feel guilty about it.

Chapter 8. How to Stop overthinking with Positive Self-talk

The practice of positive self-talk is one of the fastest ways to get out of your head. It is the practice of being optimistic and seeing the positive in just about any situation. When you can't see the positive, you are at least aware of the situation enough that it doesn't send you into a tailspin of negative thinking. You are able to see the situation for what it is.

By now, I hope you have been able to identify some of the ways that you are sabotaging your mental health and are now becoming more aware of when it occurs. Now it won't be easy to turn the negative self-talk around, but with some diligence and consistency, it is possible. It requires practice, time, and some grace toward yourself when you slip up.

What is Self-Talk?

Self-talk is the internal chatter that goes on between yourself and your brain. It's this internal chatter that can be both positive and negative, it can be distressing, and this can largely depend on your personality. If you are an optimist, then your inner dialogue will be more positive, which offers some health benefits and a better quality of life. The opposite can be said of being a pessimist, but with diligence and hard work, the negative self-talk can be turned around regardless of your personality and upbringing.

Positive self-talk has many benefits, including enhancing your general well-being, increasing your physical well-being and less stress. Other health benefits can include:

- Increased vitality

- Greater life satisfaction

- Better immune system

- Pain relief

No one really knows why this works and why people with a more positive outlook on life experience these benefits, but research suggests that these people may have the mental skills to be able to cope with stressful situations, which can reduce the harmful effects of stress.

Louise Hay, the well-known author of Heal Your Life and Heal Your Body, put this into practice when she was diagnosed with cervical cancer in 1978. She considered alternative options to surgery and instead decided to put together her own intensive program. Using affirmations, visualizations, nutritional cleansing, and psychotherapy she was able to cure her cancer completely within six months.

How to Practice

It will take time to catch the negative self-talk because it's become so ingrained in you and feels so normal, but it can be changed with practice. Once you start to recognize your patterns, then you can start to address the best practices for you.

Examples:

Negative: I failed, why did I even try? Now I'm embarrassed.

Positive: Wow! I'm proud of myself for trying something new. That was brave of me.

Negative: I've never done this before, why did I even try, I'll be so bad at it.

Positive: This is a great opportunity for me to learn something new.

Mirror talk - this may seem silly and feel awkward at first but talk to yourself in the mirror. Look yourself in the eyes and talk. Tell yourself you love yourself, that you love your hair, your eyes, whatever it is, just start talking positively to yourself about yourself.

Affirmations - write affirmations everywhere around your house. On your door as you leave the house, in kitchen drawers, on your bathroom mirror, in the car, etc. Seeing and reading these affirmations will have a positive effect on your brain and boost your serotonin, which is the 'happy' chemical in our brains because it promotes happiness and well-being.

Positive people - look at who you are surrounding yourself with, whether you believe it or not we feed off the energy of those we associate with, so find people that inspire you, lift you up, and cheer you on.

Gratitude

Given all the ideas listed throughout this book, I felt this one deserves its own heading as I strongly believe it is one of the fastest ways to turn negative self-talk into positive and set yourself up for success.

Gratitude is defined as an overall sense of feeling grateful. An emotion expressing appreciation for what you have.

It can exist as both a temporary feeling and an inherent part of who you are. Gratitude requires a recognition of something occurring that was positive and outside of you. While most of this book has been directed at healing our inner world and that is crucial to sorting through overthinking and our anxiety and depression, we also need to accept that some external forces are necessary to make us happy, but we need to show gratitude for these things.

It is generally seen as a spontaneous feeling, but it is also increasingly becoming a part of a practice to count your blessings and be grateful for what's in front of and around you. Because of this, you can deliberately cultivate a feeling of gratitude.

Gratitude Matters

It is possible to feel grateful for loved ones, colleagues, and life in general. This emotion generates an atmosphere of positivity. You will find that over time, this feeling boost happiness and promotes physical and emotional health, even when struggling with mental health obstacles. It may be a little harder to dig for the gratitude in such instances, but with practice, time and consistency you will find it is your go-to for tough times.

Practicing gratitude curbs the negative words and thoughts, and it shifts your inner attention away from anger, resentment, and jealousy, which minimizes the possibility of spiraling downward into ruminating or catastrophizing the situation.

Gratitude starts with noticing the goodness in your life, which can be hard in this world of materialism and constant comparing to others via social media, but it is possible.

It can start small, just noticing something in your day that you are grateful for, maybe it's your job because that allows you to put food on your table, or your house and having a roof over your head so you are safe, maybe it's your car because the crowding on transit makes you uncomfortable. Whatever it is, be thankful, be grateful and show it, acknowledge it. I keep a journal and write in it every morning and/or evening at least three to five things that I am grateful for that day. It has made such a difference in how I view things and react to things.

Gratitude is by far the biggest tool that has seen me through some dark
days. Being able to be grateful for any given situation knowing that it is
for my highest good has turned most of my negative self-talk and dark
thought spirals around to positive. When I catch myself slipping back
into a negative frame of mind, all I have to do is quickly list off a few
things I'm grateful for and the negativity melts away.
It wasn't always like this; it took time, practice, and consistency.

Now the real magic in gratitude that I have discovered happens when you are able to start being grateful for the people and issues in your life that challenge you. For example, you've just gone through a horrible divorce and custody battle for your children. You loathe your ex for all that he/she has put you through, but without this person, you wouldn't have your amazing kids. You realize that you are grateful to him/her for giving you such a gift. Now, I realize this may sound a little farfetched and hard to fathom, but I can speak from experience that this does work. I have recently gone through this very thing. While I am not a fan of my ex at all, I am extremely grateful for the gift of my child who wouldn't be in this world without my ex. Believe it or not, shifting to this way of thinking has made the court trips and such a little easier to deal with.

If that seems a little difficult in the beginning, then try this:

- Who has inspired you? Why?

- Keep a gratitude journal - Write big and little joys of daily life or try and identify three to five good things that happened that day.

- Try to imagine what your life would look like if some particular positive even hadn't happened.

Chapter 9.   Developing a Winning Mentality

A winning attitude is something that we develop. It is a result of the right conditioning. The same people who look so uber-confident and enthusiastic can become just the opposite of they develop a negative mentality, and the same is true vice-versa.

If you want to get out of the trap of negative thought processes and develop a winning mentality, you will have to bring some positive changes in your personality.

Given below are some small yet important changes that you must make in your day to day personal life and personality to develop a winning mentality. These changes are not very significant, yet they can leave a very deep impact on your conscious brain and the way it perceives problems. This is a thing which will matter a lot when it comes to having a winning mentality.

Start the Day with Positivity

This is a point we have already discussed in earlier chapters, but it can't be stressed enough. The way we start the day has a very deep impact on the way it will end or at least go for the most part.

If you woke up late and from the very beginning, you are worried that the day is going to be bad, you can be sure that you are correct because you have set the tone for the day. On the other hand, if you wake up smiling and leave your home expecting good things to happen, you will have many pleasant surprises in the day.

This is not some magic. When you are in a pleasant mood, even simple things look good. Have you ever felt the way day feels when you have received some very good news? On the day you are in a bad mood, even the best of the weather would mean nothing to you.

This doesn't end here. Your mood is constantly affecting your psyche. It is shouting loud and high that everything is going wrong. It has already accepted that the day has gone wrong, and it is going to end on a worse note. It would take a miracle to lift up such a mood.

Start your day on a positive note, and try to maintain it as far as possible. It would have a positive impact on your mentality.

Focus on Positivity Daily- Find at Least 4 Positive Things of the Day

At the end of the day, daily try to find at least 4 positive things about the day that has just come to its conclusion. This should be done without exception.

It can be anything that you liked on the whole day. You saw a flower, and it looked beautiful enough to lift your mood, mention it. You met a stranger who smiled at you genuinely, that can be a thing to mention. You helped someone in any way that made you feel food; this can be a thing to mention. It can be anything you liked but there should be at least 4 things that you liked about the day.

If you like, you can even journal then in a dairy or just say them out loud. This simple act can help in changing your perspective about the world. You start looking for positivity around you.

Do Something Positive for Others Daily

This is a simple act of kindness that you may do. It can be a minor act. It doesn't have to be anything major every day. But, you must do one thing at least every day that made any difference to the life of one person. When we do some act of kindness, we not only touch the lives of others, but the selfless act also touches a corner of our self too and lifts our spirit and mood.

It fills you with a sense of happiness and you feel proud of yourself either other people acknowledge it or not. It is a change that can help in infusing positivity in your mind.

Live in the Moment

You must learn to live in the present. You must stop reflecting too much on the past. Live every experience as it comes, and please stop judging things on the basis of your past experiences. This will give you a fresh perspective. Change is a reality and constant truth. The only thing that is constant is change. When we judge things on past experiences, we are coming in the way of this change.

Appreciate Yourself

This is important. You must learn to appreciate the genuine qualities in yourself. You must try to look for strong points in your personality and work on developing them. The more you appreciate yourself for your qualities, the easier it would get to break the negative thinking process.

Appreciating yourself is important if you really want to be successful in your relationships, job, and life in general. The people who are not even good enough in their own eyes can never expect to be good enough for others. If you don't appreciate yourself, you'll keep feeling stressed and insufficient. There will always be a problem with your overall satiety levels.

Find Avenues to Remain Motivated

Remaining motivated is important. You must find all the ways that are there to remain inspired and motivated. From movies to ted-talks, whatever works for you should be used to get the required push. Motivation keeps giving you the boost to continue working with the same force.

Work on Your Body Language

It is important that you work on your body language. From your clothing to the way you conduct yourself, everything in your personality should speak of your confidence and positivity. You must remember that positivity and negativity both are contagious. A positive person can light up the whole room while a negative person can make the people around gloomy. You should pick the type of person you want to be.

Remember that it is more important for you than it is important for others. Your attire, appearance, and conduct all have a deep impact on the way your mind functions.

Appreciate and Be Grateful More Often

Make it a general rule to appreciate others even for minor things that help you or make your life easy. It is another positive change that can help your mentality a lot. When you are saying positive things about others, you are reminding your mind to think in the same way. When you are expressing your gratitude for others, you are being more open, accepting, and acknowledging. This has a very deep impact on your conscious mind.

Look for Positivity Even in Grim Situations

This is a no brainer. You can't lose all hope when things start to go south. A big part of winning mentality is to maintain composure even in grim situations when others are losing hope. It is an art that needs to be developed.

Look for Solutions and Not the Problems

You must look for the problems and not the solutions. This is a statement we often hear. However, as soon as things get out of control, our mind starts looking for escape routes or even better starts exaggerating the problems. We don't contribute anything; on the contrary, we end up making things worse.

All this happens because our mind remains focused on the intensity of the problem and not on the solution. You must remember that thinking about the problem and the amount of damage it can cause can never solve it. You will have to start thinking about the way to resolve it. It is a talent that will need to be cultivated.

Conclusion

Congratulations on making it to the end of the book. It's never easy to admit that you have a problem with stress. It's something that we all experience, and it can also be something that ruins our lives. If you are not careful, then you will start to realize that stress isn't just something that you experience, but it becomes part of who you are. The longer you go without managing stress, the harder it will be to manage these feelings when you need to the most.

Remember that it is all a mental thing at first, but if not treated, it can turn into a physical problem rather quickly. Don't let the physical side of stress take over your body. You are the one in control! Not only will stress make you experience pain in your shoulders, jaw, and other parts of your body, but it will also increase your risk for more serious health conditions, such as stroke or heart attack.

What stresses you out isn't something that is going to stress others out every time either. What calms you won't calm other people. Don't compare yourself, because we all will always have differing perspectives on what is stressful, as well as how to react to our positive and negative emotions. Sometimes you might wish you could be that chill relaxed person, but remember that not everyone is always as calm as they might seem. There's nothing wrong with you if you find that you are stressed in a situation that others are completely fine. It doesn't matter what stresses you out. The most important thing is how you react to this feeling.

Always check in with yourself and ensure that you are doing your best to calm yourself at the root first. Challenge your thoughts and question your beliefs to see where the stress might have started. Just because a thought travels through your mind doesn't mean that it is true. Sometimes, we think of what we were taught to believe first, and the second thought that comes after can be what's most important.

Keep up with research on stress and anxiety as well. There will always be new ways for you to manage your stress. Since we still have yet to completely figure out our brains, there will always be emerging science around what it is that might make our brains operate in the way that they do.

Remember that everything is temporary. Everything is going to be OK in the end. You are the one that is creating stressful thoughts in your head. Sometimes you are just going to have to sit with your discomfort and feel the stress. It will end. Panic attacks will stop, and your stressful thoughts will calm down. Nothing that you experience is going to last forever.

Others say things that might stress you out, but you will always have options for how you react to these stressors. You won't always be able to stop others from causing you harm, and there will be plenty of people that will always know how to get under your skin. Though you are powerless in this, you are entirely in control of the way that you choose to handle these situations. Look for the ways that will help alleviate your stress the best.

You are not alone in the stress that you feel. Though you might feel isolated, crazy, too emotional, and plenty of other negative feelings associated with your stress, remember that this is a common emotion. You are not wrong, broken, bad, or crazy because of the emotions that you are feeling.

The things that you see online always have truth behind them. Don't let social media or inflated news articles cause you to have more stress than you already do. When you see a particularly upsetting news story, always check the sources. Take a break from your phone and really give yourself time to be quiet with your thoughts.

You might feel like you aren't doing well, but there is always going to be someone out there that is jealous or admires you. Everyone thinks that they're doing bad, but most of the time, we're doing a lot better than we'd think. Remind yourself of this in times that you are feeling more inadequate than anything.

Those who are important to you wouldn't judge you for the things that you are hard on yourself for. The ones who matter most are those people that will love you unconditionally. If anyone makes you feel bad about yourself, causing you even more stress than you initially had, remember that they are hurting. The only reason that you would want to bring someone down is because that is the way that you might already be talking to yourself! Others might still judge us, say rude things, and think negative thoughts, but that doesn't have to affect us. You know your own worth, you have your values, and you are in charge of your emotions. This is what matters the most.

You will always remember the most important things at the end of the day. When you are laying in bed alone with your thoughts, this is when you will remember the truth of your life. When everything else is stripped away - work, relationships, money, and so on, that is when your true character is revealed. You are your own person and that is beautiful!

We all have different speeds that we move through our day and in life. What you take slower might be something that others speed through. The things that you get over in a snap might be someone else's long journey. The less you compare yourself to others, the easier it will be to love yourself for who you really are.

Sometimes, you will have to laugh it off. Certain situations might be so stressful that the best thing you can do is just smile and keep pushing forward. If everything feels like it is falling apart around you, just look in the mirror and try and make the biggest grin possible.

When you are really stressed out, you can gently blow on your hands or arms. Give yourself something to fixate on, such as chewing gum or mints. Fill your home with the right kinds of colors and other things that keep you feeling good. Pick the right scents, such as lavender, to help reduce your stress. These things can seem so small, but they can really help to carry your mental health past its limits!

There are so many ways that you can reduce stress, and it is time for you to emphasize this now. It will only get worse as time goes on, so there's no better time to alleviate stress than right now!

Vagus Nerve

A Self-Help Guide To Stimulate Vagal Tone, Eliminate Anxiety and Depression With Practical Exercises To Release Your Body's Natural Ability To Heal

By

Russell Price

Introduction

You need your nerves. That much is certain. When your nerves function well, your whole body becomes capable of becoming the well-oiled machine it needs to be. The vagus nerve, however, becomes a sort of commander of most of your organs. As a cranial nerve, your vagus nerve has a very special function—it can take stimulation from your body straight to the brain without it having to go through alternate pathways. If you were to imagine all your nerves existing as a sort of transit system, complete with all sorts of stops along the way, your cranial nerves would be like the express routes. They get you from point A to B without having to go between other intermediaries. While other signals throughout your body will route back through your spinal cord, your vagus nerve is a direct line of travel from the body to the brain.

We are going to be discussing the vagus nerve, learning how it works and what you can expect from it. When you understand how your vagus nerve works and why it matters, you can begin to identify the areas in which your life may have been impacted by it in some way. You may be surprised to find out that, all along, you had a low vagal tone, implying that your vagus nerve is not firing properly. Your vagal tone is the way in which we determine how functional that vagus nerve is. While it can be checked through directly connecting to the vagus nerve to identify just how much activity is occurring within it, there are other methods that you can use as well. You can discover the health of your vagus nerve through the variation in your heart rate during your inhales and exhales. When there is a larger variation between the inhale and exhale, it is believed that the vagus nerve is more powerful—it is referred to as toned. When you see very little variability, however, you may have other secondary problems occurring as well, and that is when you want to start considering interventions to help support it.

The vagus nerve is a pair of cranial nerves that originate from the base of the brainstem. They travel down from the brainstem in several different branches that reach across much of the body. This nerve is named vagus from the same root word of vagabond—it means wanderer. Aptly named, the vagus nerve travels throughout the face, the neck, the torso, and the abdomen, innervating several different areas and influencing how they work.

In particular, the vagus nerve is sensorimotor. This means that, while most nerves are specialized one way or the other, the vagus nerve has the capability to communicate both to and from the brain. It allows for sensation and sensory data to be taken to the brain, which is where the afferent nature comes into play. However, it also sends commands from the brain to the rest of the body to control it, which is where it gets its efferent ability. It can not only sense but moves the body around you.

As a rule, if you need to remember between afferent and efferent, try using this quick mnemonic: afferent nerves arrive at the brain with their information while efferent nerves exit the brain with their information. Afferent nerves are your sensory nerves that would need to be able to send information straight to the brain in order to have it processed properly. Efferent nerves are your motor nerves that are responsible for moving your muscles and controlling your body, even if the muscles that are being moved are the involuntary muscles of your organs that keep you alive.

This nerve, however, is important just since it is so widely reaching and due to the wide range of the control it has over the body. It is intricately involved in your emotional regulation, determining how you handle stress and how you interact with other people. It is responsible for ensuring that you are capable of functioning thanks to the intermediary that it plays between all these important body parts and the brain.

You can see the vagus nerve serving as a sort of regulator of the autonomic nervous system. It allows for the fear responses that people have. That fear response is what the body needs to be ready and able to interact with the world. Think about it—if you had to consciously consider the pros and cons of running away from a tiger instead of fighting the tiger off, there is a good chance that you would spend so much time deliberating between the two that instead, you would wind up getting attacked long before you made a decision. Because of that, the vagus nerve takes control for you. It makes these sorts of snap-decisions for you, so you do not have to make them instead. It removes that delay of having to consciously decide what you do so you can react instinctively. You respond with that same primal part of your brain that will lead other animals to react to their surroundings. You will usually either fight, run away, or freeze up altogether, but it happens without you making the decision yourself in order to save you crucial time that will otherwise be better spent keeping you alive.

Chapter 1 What is Vagus Nerve and Where is it?

The vagus nerve is the longest of the cranial nerves and is functionally one of the most important nerves in the body. Heart rate, digestion, blood pressure, sweating, and even vocal function are some of the vital physiological processes that are regulated by the vagus nerve. It is the main link for the transmission of information between the brain and other body organs and tissues. The vagus nerve, therefore, facilitates the monitoring of various organ systems by the brain.

The Structure Of The Vagus Nerve

The Vagus Nerve derives its name from the Latin term vagary that alludes to its wandering and long structure that extends from the head to the abdomen. It is the longest and most complex of the 12 cranial nerves. It travels through the jugular foramen, passes into the carotid sheath between the internal carotid artery and the internal jugular vein below the head, to the neck, chest, and abdomen, where it facilitates the innervation of the viscera.

From the medulla of the brain stream, the vagus nerve exits the cranium through the jugular foramen, which is in the base of the skull. Within the skull, the auricular branch of the Vagus nerve arises to provide a sensory response to the auditory canal as well as the external ear. From the head, the vagus nerve then extends to the neck through the carotid sheath.

The vagus nerve, while in the neck will travel inferiorly with the jugular vein and the carotid until the base of the neck at which point the right and left vagus nerve branch into two different pathways. The right vagus nerve enters the thorax by passing anteriorly to the subclavian artery and posteriorly to the sternoclavicular joint. In contrast, the left vagus nerve will enter the thorax, passing posteriorly to the sternoclavicular joint and between the carotid and left subclavian arteries.

While in the neck the Vagus nerve branches into;

- The superior laryngeal nerve consisting of internal and external branches. The external branch of the laryngeal nerve provides sensory innervation for the larynx through the cricothyroid muscle.

- The pharyngeal branch which provides motor innervation to muscles of the soft palate and pharynx.

- The recurrent laryngeal nerve extends from the right subclavian artery to the larynx and function in innervating the muscles of the larynx.

Once the vagus nerve gets to the chest, it branches into the posterior vagal trunk and the anterior vagal trunk. The anterior vagal trunk arises from the left vagus nerve, while the posterior vagal trunk arises from the right vagus nerve. The smooth muscles of the esophagus are innervated by the esophageal plexus, which is formed by these vagal trunks.

The cardiac branches which also arise in the thorax function in the innervation of the heart muscles regulating the heart rate. Most of the muscles of the larynx are innervated by the left recurrent laryngeal nerve. The vagal trunks from the thorax extend to the abdomen through an opening in the diaphragm, referred to as the esophageal hiatus.

While in the abdomen, the vagal trunks divide into multiple branches that supply the small and large bowels, the stomach, and the esophagus.

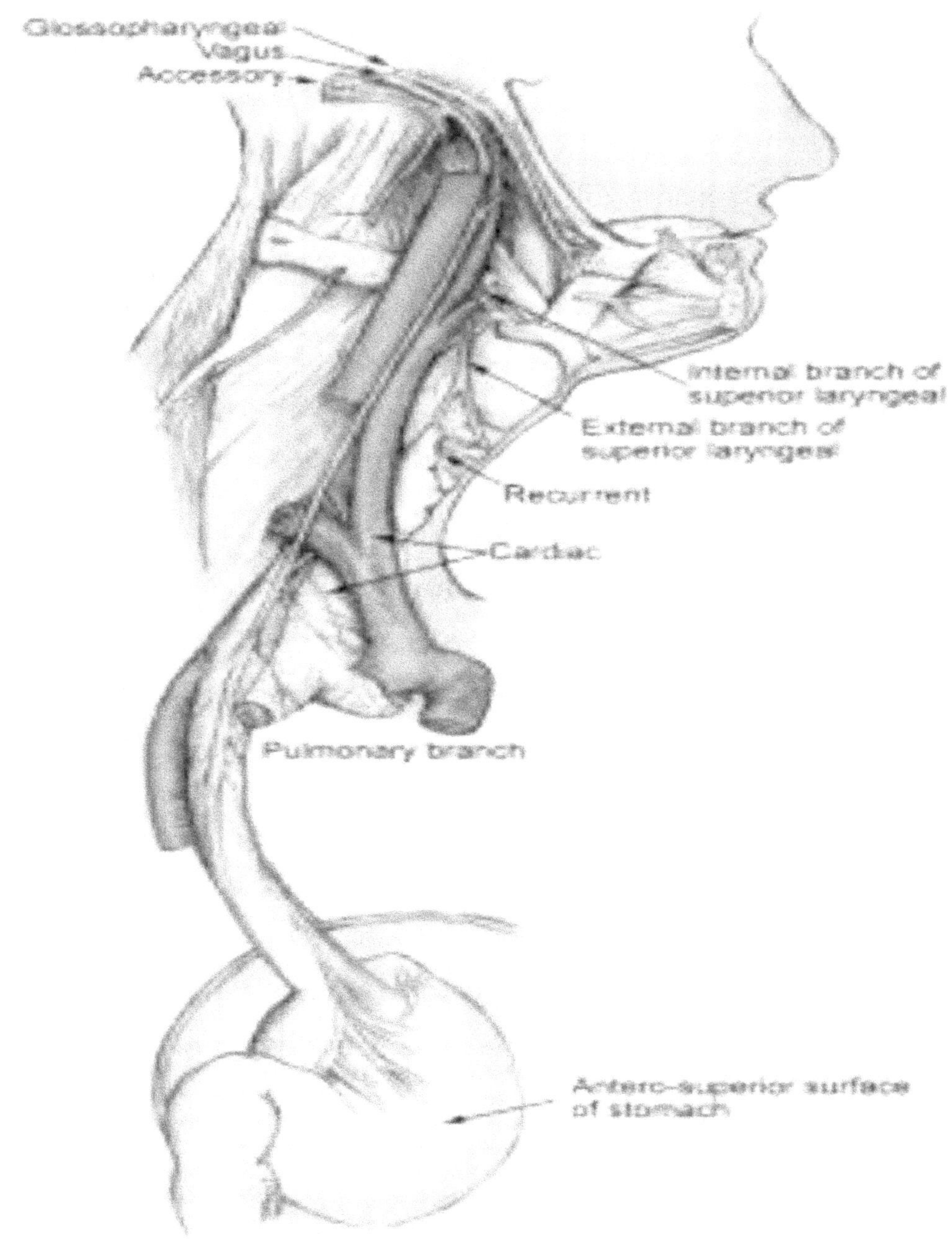

The Functions Of The Vagus Nerve

The vagus nerve is a mixed cranial nerve that has both sensory and motor functions. The sensory functions of the vagus nerve can be either somatic or visceral in nature. Sensations felt on the skin or in the muscles are typically somatic, while those felt in the body organs are visceral.

The sensory functions of the Vagus nerve include;

•	Supplying visceral sensation to the heart, lungs, digestive system, trachea, esophagus, and the larynx.

•	Providing somatic sensation to parts of the throat and the ear canal.

•	The sensation of taste at the base of the tongue

The motor functions of the vagus nerve include;

• The vagus nerve innervates heart muscles, thereby regulating the heart rate.

• The vagus nerve facilitates peristalsis or the movement of food through the digestive tract by stimulating contractions in the esophagus, stomach, and in the intestines.

• The vagus nerve stimulates muscles in the larynx, pharynx, and the soft palate.

The greatest significance of the vagus nerve when it comes to health is that it is the body's major parasympathetic nerve. This means that it supplies parasympathetic fibers to all the major organs in the head, neck, and chest, as well as the abdomen.

The vagus nerve is responsible for involuntary parasympathetic responses and is in control of functions such as the gag reflex, sneezing, and coughing reflexes. Afferent vagus nerve fibers that stimulate the pharynx and back of the throat stimulate the gag reflex. In fact, doctors will often check vagal activity by testing the gag reflex by tickling the back of the throat with a soft cotton swab, if this test fails to elicit gagging in the patient; it serves as an indicator of vagus nerve dysfunction.

Other physiological functions that are regulated by the vagus nerve include; slowing down the heart rate, regulating sweating, controlling blood pressure, and even peristalsis, which is the movement of food in the gastrointestinal tract to facilitate digestion.

By creating a crucial link for the brain to organ and organ to brain communication, the vagus nerve enables the brain to regulate different processes and organ functions to ensure that the body is maintained in the ideal homeostatic state. For our organs to function properly, processes need to be inhibited or activated depending on our internal or external environment.

Take, for instance, a person who is jogging. Their energy demands will be high in order to sustain physical activity. This will require the heart to beat faster, pumping more blood to the muscles so that they get enough oxygen. Now let's consider someone who is taking a nap, their energy demand is low since the body is in a rested state, and hence their heart rate will be slower because the energy demand by the body is low.

In effect, your body needs to adjust to your internal and external state appropriately to the internal and external environment in order to remain in optimum health. The vagus nerve plays an important afferent role by bringing information from the internal organs such as the heart, lungs, and gut to the brain. Moreover, it also functions in an efferent role where it mitigates the effects of the sympathetic nervous system.

The vagus nerve in its parasympathetic role is a big determinant of how well the internal homeostasis or balance in the body is maintained. The fight and flight responses that are activated by the sympathetic system during times of stress or danger need to be effectively switched off or inhibited once the threat has been resolved; this is where the parasympathetic role of the vagus nerve comes in.

As we have seen, fight or flight responses are our bodies' way of preparing us to fight threats. Without these responses, our lives would be short because we would not have adequate self-defense mechanisms. Look at it this way, without the adrenaline rush that comes with fear. You may not be able to outrun that aggressive dog or fight off an aggressor. By increasing your energy reserves by elevating your heart rate, breathing rate, and even reducing your sensitivity to pain, the fight and flight responses enable you to defend yourself from threats.

However, what happens after the threat has been resolved, and you are no longer in danger? Your body needs to return to a rested state for normal body function to resume. This is achieved when the vagus nerve in its parasympathetic role inhibits the fight and flight responses and restores the body to a rested state.

The vagus nerve effectively puts the body back in a relaxed or rested state by slowing down the heartbeat, decreasing the rate of respiration, and stimulating digestive function. These interventions by the vagus nerve ensure that once a threat has been resolved, your body is reverted to a relaxed and rested state.

Without the proper functioning of the vagus nerve, the sympathetic nervous system becomes overstimulated, and this, in turn, causes disorders in the body. To ensure that our vagal activity is high, there are measures we can take to routinely stimulate and activate its parasympathetic effects and ensure that we reap the benefits of the healing power of this powerful nerve.

The Vagus Nerve and Good Health

While we can understand the functions of the vagus nerve in the body, it is even more important to relate these functions to our physical and mental health and understand the role of the vagus nerve in maintaining physical and psychological health.

Cardiovascular Health

The vagus nerve plays a crucial role in ensuring normal cardiovascular function. The vagus nerve regulates the heart rate in effect functioning as a natural pacemaker. By stimulating the cardiac muscles, the vagus nerve can effectively slow down our heart rate when it is too fast, as happens in stressful conditions. When the heart rate is increased, it can lead to the elevation of the blood pressure, which causes strain on the heart tissue and blood vessels.

Research has shown that a decrease in vagal activity or vagal tone is linked to an increase in mortality when it comes to heart failure conditions. By regulating the heart rate, the vagus nerve can effectively reduce blood pressure and by extension, reduces damage to the cardiac muscles. A properly functioning vagus nerve is, therefore, crucial for cardiovascular health and in avoiding conditions such as hypertension.

Chronic Inflammation

Have you ever noticed that redness, swelling, or even pus that occurs when you injure yourself? Notice how, when you fall and scrape your knees or stub your toe, the affected area becomes swollen and red? These are all indicators of inflammation that we routinely experience.

Inflammation is an essential part of the immune system's reaction to physical injury or pathogenic infection in the body. Inflammation signals the immune system to heal and repair injured tissue and defend itself against pathogens such as bacteria and other disease-causing pathogens. Without inflammation as a defense mechanism, wounds would not heal, and even minor infections could prove fatal.

On the flip side, when an inflammatory response is prolonged for extended periods of time, the body begins to attack its cells. This is referred to as chronic inflammation. In fact, chronic inflammation is an underlying cause in diseases such as heart disease, stroke, and autoimmune disorders, including rheumatoid arthritis and lupus.

What this means is that while inflammation is a natural part of the healing process, when it goes on uninhibited for extended periods of time, it can cause severe health problems. The vagus nerve becomes instrumental in managing chronic inflammation because of its parasympathetic responses that can effectively inhibit the sympathetic responses of fight or flight. When your vagal activity or tone is strong, the vagus nerve can effectively inhibit inflammatory responses and prevent overstimulation of the immune system.

On the other hand, a reduced vagal tone results in the secretion of pro-inflammatory cytokines and ultimately causes an increase in sympathetic nervous system responses that are linked to chronic inflammation.

The vagus nerve can effectively control inflammation by inhibiting the overstimulation of the immune system that is caused by the sympathetic nervous system. Medical research has shown that stimulation of the vagus nerve helps in managing conditions that are related to prolonged inflammation of tissues in the body. Vagal stimulation has been found to be effective as a therapy in managing pain in rheumatoid arthritis and other autoimmune disorders.

Weight Management

Ever wondered where some people could feel full after eating only a small portion of food while others take longer to feel satiated? Well, this phenomenon is linked to the sensitivity of the vagus nerve. The more sensitive your vagus nerve is, the quicker you feel full when eating, and the lower the sensitivity of the vagus nerve, the longer it will take you to feel full.

But how does this come about? The answer lies in the gut-brain axis, which is the connection between the brain and the gut. The link and communication between these two organs are facilitated by the vagus nerve. The vagus nerve is the main communication channel between the gastrointestinal tract and the brain. This means that the efficacy of the vagus nerve function will have an impact on various factors, including:

- Digestion

- Weight gain or weight loss

In a scenario where the vagal tone is decreased, it loses the sensitivity that enables it to detect and communicate to the brain that the stomach is full. The net result of this is overeating, which inevitably leads to weight gain and digestive disorders.

An increased vagal tone means that the vagus nerve will have a higher sensitivity to the fullness signal from the gut, and this means that you will tend to feel full faster and on less food. This is essential in weight management because most people struggling with weight management tend to consume more calories than the body requires. Therefore, the less you eat, the easier it is to keep the excess pounds off.

Stress Management

Stress is one of the leading causes of ill health in the world today. From physical to psychological disorders, stress is a major underlying cause of poor health. When we think of fight and flight responses, it is easy to assume that they are only triggered by physical threats. This is not true. Whether your stress is emotional or physical, the body's response is to activate the fight or flight mode to enable you to resolve the imminent threat or stress factor.

When you are anxious about work, worrying about your children, or even fretting about the daily pressures of life, your sympathetic nervous system perceives a threat and triggers the fight or flight response. This means that when you are dealing with chronic stress or anxiety, the flight or fight responses are perpetually turned on. This, as we have seen, can lead to chronic inflammation, autoimmune disorders, and a myriad of health complications.

Since the vagus nerve can effectively inhibit the fight or flight responses, it can easily restore the body to a rest and relaxed state. This means that it will counteract the fight or flight responses, such as the release of cortisol, which has been linked to weight, gain, insomnia, and even hypertension. The vagus nerve helps in combating stress because it can stop the fight and flight responses that are triggered when you are stressed, anxious, or in danger.

A common technique used in managing anxiety and even anger is taking slow and deep breaths. The mechanism behind this is that deep breathing activates the vagus nerve and enables it to restore the body to a relaxed and rested state. This is crucial when it comes to stress management. People with poor vagal activity are prone to chronic stress and depressive tendencies because their fight and flight response system are not being sufficiently kept in check by the vagus nerve.

Proper Breathing

One of the effects of Vagus nerve activity is in controlling our respiration rate through its effect on the bronchioles. The Vagus nerve facilitates proper breathing through the neurotransmitter acetylcholine. Proper breathing is not only an effective way to deal with pain but is also effective in coping with stress by creating a calming effect on the body.

Since the vagus nerve is connected to the diaphragm, it is possible to stimulate it by doing deep abdominal breathing or holding your breath for six to seven counts. Relaxation techniques such as meditation and yoga incorporate breathing techniques because proper breathing has a relaxing effect on the body.

Improved memory

Stimulation of the vagus nerve has been found to affect improving memory and cognitive ability. When the vagus nerve is stimulated, it triggers the release of the neurotransmitter norepinephrine into the amygdala, which forms part of the limbic system. This means that the activation of the vagus nerve can be beneficial in counteracting and managing the effects of some cognitive disorders such as Alzheimer's.

Chapter 2 How to Activate and Access the Power of the Vagus Nerve

Simulating the vagus nerve can be a bit more difficult than it sounds. This nerve runs through almost every major organ, from the brain to the colon (Roland, 2019).

Many of the techniques for stimulating the vagus nerve requires one's full body. Yoga, for example, is an amazing way to stimulate the vagus nerve. Not only does it soothe and calm almost all the major organs, but positions that stretch the spine and neck directly stimulate the nerve itself (Spindler, 2018). The lungs and heart are both healed and soothed by the deep breathing and physical activity of yoga (Spindler, 2018).

You can think about vagus nerve healing as physical, mental, emotional, or even spiritual. Spiritual practices like meditation stimulate the nerve just as readily as more physical activities. Regardless of your own spiritual beliefs, ideas about positive and negative energy, mindfulness, and interconnectedness have a great deal of validity when we look at how the vagus nerve works. Whether you want to think about these exercises as improving the neurological functions of the nerve or allowing positive energy to flow through the body, the result (and the basic underlying idea) is the same.

Different exercises will work for different people. Everyone is trying to heal, recover, or prevent something different. However, I encourage you to try each of these exercises at least once, no matter how strange or unrelated to your healing journey they may seem. It may seem "new age" to think that something like sound healing or aromatherapy could help you to manage something cancer or MS, but you might be amazed by how much better you feel.

Most of the exercises given in this chapter will be things that you can do at home, or without the help of a professional. However, there are many therapies and techniques that require the intervention of a licensed professional that will also stimulate the vagus nerve. There are also some therapies that you can choose to do by yourself or with a professional. Yoga, for example, is something you can do at home with a book or following a YouTube channel. Or you can find a local studio and take classes with a licensed professional. The choice is yours!

However, as a reference, here is a more complete list of activities that can help you to stimulate the vagus nerve, sorted into the four healing categories of physical, mental, emotional, and spiritual. All of us will naturally gravitate to one of these four healing techniques. Of the four may seem most appropriate for your own healing journey. This is perfectly natural. However, I do encourage you to try at least one technique from all four categories to begin approaching your health and wellness from a more holistic place.

Physical (Atkinson, 2019)

- Exercise

- Speed walking

- Stretching

- Yoga

- Massage therapies

- Detoxification

- Activated charcoal

- Skin brushing and saunas

- Gallbladder flush

- Herbs and herbal supplements

- Eating plant-based, whole foods

- Drinking water

- Nutritional supplements

- Limit alcohol

- Limit caffeine

- Hot baths

- Cold showers

- Go outside

- Get enough sleep

- Aromatherapy

Mental (Psychological) (Atkinson, 2019)

- Affirmations

- Brain balance

- Visualizations and goal setting

- Biofeedback

- Journaling

- Talk therapy

- Cognitive behavioral therapy

- Psychotherapy

- Limit social media engagement

- Positive social interactions

  - Hobbies or activities that are purely done for fun

Emotional

- Listening to and/or playing music

- Emotional freedom techniques

- Cultivate a positive attitude

- Self-comforting techniques

- Letting go

- Relaxation techniques

- Practicing gratitude

- Self-rewarding

- Decompression

- Grounding techniques

- Hypnosis

  - Lifestyle changes to eliminate negative people or situations

Spiritual

- Yoga

- Sound healing

- Biofeedback

- Meditation

- Mindfulness

- Aromatherapy

- Spiritual healing (of any religious or spiritual belief)

- Crystal healing

- Prayer or spiritual ritual

- Chakra healing

  - Connecting with nature

Many of these techniques seem simple, even too simple. But remember how the vagus nerve works. Polyvagal theory teaches us that the vagus nerve shuts down when it perceives that we are in danger. It begins to fire different signals to ensure that we survive whatever is threatening our safety. However, when our bodies are chronically in the danger state, the vagus nerve remains dysfunctional for long periods of time, and we never enter the state of recovery and healing that necessarily follows a period of danger. Every exercise or technique that stimulates the vagus nerve is meant to bring your body out of the danger state, which means convincing the body and/or mind that you are in a place of safety.

If you have multiple illnesses, it will take longer for any of these healing activities to take effect. Be patient with yourself and your body and continue to work with your doctor or other medical professionals to manage your symptoms while you are engaging in these healing activities.

Measuring Vagus Nerve Function

It can sometimes feel like every major illness you can think of is caused by vagus nerve dysfunction. But the vagus nerve is not the only factor in our health and wellness. Therefore, as you are being working with the vagus nerve, it's important to measure its function, so that you can determine what illness are caused by the vagus nerve, and what illness are triggered by other causes.

The first, and most common, way to measure vagus nerve function is by measuring your vagal tone. To do this, breathe in deeply, and then slowly breathe out. Count your heartbeats as you breathe in and count them again as you breathe out. You should end up with two numbers, that you can put one over the other. Your vagal tone will look something like this: 9/6. That's nine heartbeats while breathing in, and six heartbeats breathing out.

The bigger the difference between these two numbers, the better your vagal tone. So, for example, 9/4 is better than 9/6. The reason that we can use such a system is because your heart rate speeds up slightly when you breathe in and slows down when you breathe out. The more your heart can slow, the easier it is for your body to calm down after stimulation. If your body is unable to calm itself down, this is a primary indicator that the vagus nerve has been compromised and is regulating the body in a state of stress, no matter how relaxed you may feel.

This slight speeding up and slowing down of the heart with each breath is called respiratory sinus arrhythmia, or RSA. When using this method to measure vagal tone, however, there are a few things to keep in mind. Your RSA (and, by extension, your vagal tone) is higher when lying down than when sitting up. You can choose to measure your RSA either way, but if you are trying to track its improvement, make sure that you are always in the same position when taking a reading. For example, if you take your first reading lying down, when you check again, you should also make sure that you're lying down.

It's also important to note that RSA declines naturally with age, and that there is to flat acceptable rate for RSA. In other words, everyone's heart beats slightly differently. If you are using RSA to measure vagal functionality, it's best to use it as a measure of your improvement, rather than relying on it as a judgment of whether your vagus nerve is working properly. In other words, no matter where your RSA is at the beginning of the month, after four weeks of consistently working to stimulate the vagus nerve, you should notice an increase in your RSA at the end of the month.

A less exact method of measuring vagus nerve function is by measuring heart rate variability. Most of the nerves responsible for regulating the heart's pace making activity are vagus nerves, which means trouble with the heartbeat almost always indicates dysfunction of the vagus nerve. A healthy heart should beat between 60-100 times per minute. If your heartbeat is faster than this while you are sitting and resting, this could indicate dysfunction of the vagus nerve.

Believe it or not, the time between each heartbeat isn't exact. Furthermore, it shouldn't be exact. While there is such a thing as an irregular heartbeat (which can also indicate trouble with the vagus nerve), a healthy heart should have a slight variation in the time between each beat. This slight variation is called heart variability. Strange as it may sound, your heartbeat can be too regular.

Low heart variability isn't a health condition in and of itself. But it's a sign that our body is operating under a certain level of stress. When we are in danger, our heart beats faster, but it also beats with more regularity. It begins to pound at a strong, steady pace, pumping oxygenated blood to our organs and muscles as fast as possible. When we come back to a state of safety, the heart will then relax, and return to its normal, slightly offbeat rhythm. This change in pace is almost entirely regulated by the vagus nerve. Therefore, low heart variability almost certainly indicates trouble with the vagus nerve.

There are other ways to measure vagal tone, but they aren't as easy to do at home. For example, the heart makes a sound when it beats. Measuring the frequency of your heartbeat is also a reliable indicator of vagal tone (sometimes called vagal sound when measured in this way). A healthy heart should measure between 0.15 and 0.4 Hz. Anything else indicates trouble with the heart, and specifically with its pace making activity. This, in turn, implicates trouble with the vagus nerve as well.

Vagal tone is being measured by an increasing number of healthcare professionals, especially in young children. It may not surprise you to learn that people with low vagal tone are typically at a much higher risk for psychological issues like emotional regulation, anxiety, internalizing disorders, and externalizing disorders. However, as the relationship between brain and body becomes more apparent, the link between vagal tone and physical health problems is steadily becoming clearer. Vagal tone is increasingly being measured in children diagnosed with autism. Children with high vagal tone also tend to exhibit more empathetic responsiveness and less social inhibition than children with low vagal tone.

Basic Exercises to Activate the Vagus Nerve

Find the exercises that work for you! All of them work, and all of them work well. For optimum stimulation of the vagus nerve, do at least two minutes of breathing exercises and ten minutes of physical exercise every day.

Breathing Exercises

Valsalva Maneuver

Take a deep breath in. Now close your mouth, pinch your nose, and gently breathe out. Hold this for a moment, and then release your nose to let out your breath. This technique will create a gentle pressure in the chest cavity, which, in turn, stimulates the vagus nerves connected to the lungs and airways.

Diaphragmatic Breathing

 The diaphragm is a bell-shaped muscle located directly beneath the lungs. When you inhale, the muscle flattens out, acting as a kind of pump to allow the lungs to expand. When you breathe from the diaphragm, you breathe deeply to fill the chest. You'll notice your stomach expands outward, and contracts when you exhale.

There are two basic ways to breathe from the diaphragm. The first is to simply breathe! Sit in a quiet place with your back straight. Sit either in a cross-legged position, or with the feet planted firmly on the floor. Take a deep breath, making a conscious effort to fill the chest with air. Hold it for a moment, and then breathe out. Do this for at least two minutes.

The other way is to sing! For your lungs to get enough air to sing, you must breathe from the diaphragm. So, when you start to sing, you automatically breathe from the diaphragm. Otherwise, you wouldn't have enough air to push through your vocal cords and no sound would come out. Put on a song you like and sing along. If you do this every day, you're giving your diaphragm a good workout and you're giving your vagus nerve both psychological and physical stimulation.

Audible Breathing

Normally your breath is silent. When your exhale is audible, however, it means that the glottis is partially closed. The glottis is located at the back of your tongue. The vagus nerve is connected to the glottis and stimulating this part of the tongue stimulates the vagus nerve.

For audible breathing exercises, find a quiet place to sit with your back straight. Sit in a cross-legged position or sit with your feet planted firmly on the floor. Take a deep breath and hold it for a moment. When you exhale, sigh or hiss out your breath. Think of the sound you made as a child to breathe on a cold window in order to fog it up. Breathe in this way for at least two minutes.

7-11 Diaphragmatic Breathing Exercise (Turner, 2019)

Find a quiet place to sit with your back straight. Sit with your legs crossed or your feet planted firmly on the floor. Inhale through your nose, filling the chest cavity with air, and count to seven. Hold your breath for one second, then exhale audibly through the mouth, making a sigh or a hissing sound. Exhale for a count of 11. This is one cycle. Repeat this for six-12 cycles a day.

Obstructed Diaphragmatic Breathing Exercise

Find a quiet place to sit with your back straight. Sit with your legs crossed or your feet planted firmly on the floor. Inhale through your nose, filling the chest cavity with air, until you can't take in even one more drop of air. Then purse your lips and exhale forcefully, almost as if you are blowing all the air out of your lungs. Do this until you can't exhale any more. This is one cycle. Repeat this for 6-12 cycles a day.

Physical Exercises

Walking

Going for a walk 30-60 minutes a day is a very easy way to stimulate the vagus nerve. It's not just the physical activity that makes this exercise so effective. Exposure to sunlight and fresh air also stimulate the brain and sensory nerves. Walking stimulates the heart and blood vessels and breathing in the fresh air stimulates and lungs and airways. If you are walking at a quick pace, 30 minutes will do. If you want to go slow and take your time, it's better to go for about an hour. If it's cold outside, dress warmly and walk anyway. Cold air on the face has been found to stimulate the vagus nerve, though it's still unclear why. It may have something to do with the connection between the nerve and the facial muscles. Either way, a brisk winter wind and cold air in the lungs is a great stimulating supplement to the cardiovascular activity of walking.

High-Intensity Interval Sprinting

High-intensity interval sprinting stimulates the vagus nerve by waking up the heart and lungs. Doing these one to two times a week will provide the necessary stimulation to the nerve.

To do this exercise, run as fast as you possibly can for 30 seconds, and then walk for two minutes. This is one cycle. Repeat this cycle for just 10 minutes to get a full workout.

Cardio Machines

Treadmills or other walking machines at the gym are great if you don't have a good place to walk outdoors. Especially for those who live in cold climates, taking advantage of a treadmill at the gym or even investing in one for the home is a good way to keep you walking every day, indoors or out.

Jump Rope

Did you ever jump or skip rope as a child? Believe it or not, this childhood game is a great way to get your heart beating and your lungs expanding with fresh air. Find a simple child's jump rope and jump for two to five minutes a day to stimulate the vagus nerve. This can be done indoors (of course), but if you can, try to do it outside to get the extra benefits of fresh air and sun exposure.

Chapter 3 Inflammation, and Diseases Associated with Vagus Nerve

Nearly every autoimmune disease is caused by inflammation in the body. In fact, a great number of diseases, in general, are due to inflammation in the tissues. It is a big problem and one that pills can't really fix, though anti-inflammatories will lower it somewhat.

Inflammation has been linked to some of the deadliest diseases today, including diabetes, cancer, stroke, heart disease, and others. It has also been connected to autism and mental health issues, as well as several other brain diseases. Inflammation can kill you, but it's not entirely bad.

A study done by Dr. Harold A. Silverman at the Laboratory for Biomedical Science at the Feinstein Institute for Medical Research showed some interesting connections between inflammation and the vagus nerve. It showed that if the vagus nerve has a low tone, then the body is at higher risk for increased and chronic inflammation. This prolonged inflammation could cause issues like rheumatoid arthritis and other conditions associated with long term inflammation in the body.

What Is Inflammation?

Before we look further at how the vagus nerve influences inflammation, you should understand what inflammation all is about. It's an essential part of the immune system, so in small doses, it is something you want to happen in the body, to a certain point. Sometimes it seems to overload, and that's when it becomes too much to handle.

Inflammation is when the tissues swell and redden. They may become hot to the touch, as well. It is the natural immune response to something irritating.

For example, if you get a splinter in your skin, it is viewed as a foreign object and an irritant. Your immune system responds by inflaming the idea to help the body expel and rid itself of the irritant.

However, irritants aren't just actual foreign bodies. They can be germs, bacteria, viruses, or even medications or treatments for other diseases, like chemicals, chemotherapy, or radiation. Specific areas of inflammation have names, usually ending in "itis" such as dermatitis, which is inflammation of the skin, or bronchitis, which is an inflammation of the bronchi.

Symptoms get worse as the inflammation gets worse. It will start out with heat, swelling, pain, and redness, moving on to loss of function of the area that is affected. An inflamed joint will become impossible to move, and inflamed bronchi will make it tough to breathe.

As the inflammation worsens, you will start to feel sick and tired. A fever may occur, as well, another sign that your immune system is working overtime to eliminate the disease that has invaded. Your body will pour all energy into fighting the bacteria or virus, and the fever raises your metabolism, making it possible for the body to produce more antibodies and white blood cells.

Blood vessels tend to dilate to allow more blood flow to the affected area, which is necessary to get the white blood cells to the area of inflammation. This also causes a lot of pain, which is another protective mechanism. You will tend not to move a body part that is hurting, and you'll keep it protected.

The swelling that becomes evident at the site of infection is due to more and more fluid and blood cells rushing to the area. Once the irritant has been dealt with, the fluid level drops, and the swelling goes down. You will notice this, particularly in the nose when you have a cold or flu. The extra fluid helps eliminate the viruses, but it makes it hard to breathe through your nose when it is all swollen inside, thanks to inflammation of the mucous membranes.

When there is an actual threat to the body, this immune system response is invaluable and could even save your life. Unfortunately, inflammation isn't always helpful, and if it occurs outside an actual threat, it can cause a lot of issues. In fact, it is the main reason we have an autoimmune disease, which is when the body's immune system mistakes its own cells for an intruder and fights against it.

While it started out as a part of a healthy, functioning body, inflammation has become rampant in our lives for a variety of reasons. The SAD (standard American diet) that so many enjoy triggers inflammation throughout the body. Things like sugar, processed grains, and food additives can all contribute to this. In addition, people use more medications than ever before. As I've mentioned, this was my personal trigger for vagus nerve damage, but it all starts with inflammation.

The problem here is that inflammation and chronic sickness create a terrible cycle. The illness creates inflammation, and the inflammation worsens the illness. Add in all the other factors in life that are contributing to the inflammation of everything, and you have a serious problem that is very difficult to fix.

How Much Inflammation is Too Much?

Since inflammation is obviously a very important part of the immune system, you don't want to eradicate it completely. When do you know that it's too much? That's the big question that everyone wants to know the answer to.

If you are sick, some inflammation is normal. For example, when your nasal membranes swell up as you have a cold, it's a normal part of fighting off the virus. This isn't overkilling, and it will help your body recover faster. The same goes for when you are injured. A scraped knee will tend to get red and swollen for a day or two, then it subsides. If your immune system is doing its job properly, you don't have to worry.

The problem starts when things get out of hand. If you're not sick or injured, but you are experiencing inflammatory responses, something may be wrong. When multiple body parts become inflamed for apparently no reason, it can also be an indication that the immune system is malfunctioning. Where it may be normal for one knee to swell up due to an injury, even one you don't recall happening, it's not normal for your shoulders, knees, and wrists to swell, heat up, and get red. This would probably indicate an overload of inflammatory hormones.

Another indication that it may be too much inflammation is when it lasts longer than the average disease. Inflammatory symptoms that continue far beyond the usual 3-7 days for a virus or several days or weeks past what would be normal for an injury can indicate a poorly functioning immune system.

Your doctor can help you diagnose an inflammatory issue since it will also tend to show up in blood tests. However, your own experiences can also tell you if you have a problem. You know your body best and will be able to determine if there is something going on with it.

Autoimmune Diseases Caused by Inflammation

Once the body starts fighting its own cells, a war begins in you. This can be horribly uncomfortable, but it gets worse. When your immune system is busy fighting off an imaginary threat, it is more susceptible to other diseases sneaking in. You may find that if you suffer from an autoimmune disease, you also deal with a lot of colds and flu. You may feel like you catch every bug going by, and that's because you do. When the immune system is fighting this hard, it can't stop everything, and germs will get past the lowered protective barriers.

Autoimmune diseases are varied in how they present, but they all have one thing in common . . . the immune system is fighting against your own body. Here are some of the more common diseases associated with this issue.

Addison's disease: The adrenal glands are the affected organs in this disease. They produce several hormones, including androgen, aldosterone, and cortisol. Without these, the body can become quite imbalanced. You'll tend to lose weight, feel weak and exhausted, and your blood sugar will usually below. This also causes excess potassium to wind up in the blood, while sodium levels drop drastically.

Autoimmune vasculitis: When the immune system attacks blood vessels, it can cause serious issues. The resulting inflammation squeezes the arteries and veins, nearly closing them and preventing proper circulation. This causes some pretty obvious health risks that should be avoided.

Celiac disease: Also referred to as gluten sensitivity, this is an autoimmune disease where gluten causes the immune system to attack the small intestine when passing through. This results in inflammation and can cause leaky gut. It's a very serious disease, and even a small amount of gluten can trigger an immune response.

Grave's disease: This autoimmune disease causes the thyroid to overproduce hormones. Too many thyroid hormones will speed up your metabolism and can speed up your heart rate, cause extreme weight loss, anxiety, and heat intolerance. One of the most notable and unpleasant symptoms of Grave's disease is eyes that bulge out of the head.

Hashimoto's: You may have heard of this disease, which also affects the thyroid. However, unlike Grave's, Hashimoto's causes the thyroid to stop functioning properly, and it has the opposite effect on the body, causing weight gain. You'll tend to be sensitive to cold, and your hair will fall out. It can also cause goiters, or the swelling of the thyroid to the point that it forms a large lump on the neck.

Inflammatory bowel disease: Commonly known as IBD, there are a few sub-diseases under this. It refers to inflammation of the intestinal walls, but depending on where it is, the disease has a specific name.

Crohn's disease affects any part of the digestive tract, even outside the intestines. It can cause inflammation from anus to mouth, though it generally only affects a certain section of the GI tract.

Ulcerative colitis is specifically limited to the colon and rectum and is caused by massive inflammation there.

Lupus: Systemic lupus erythematosus is another autoimmune disease that you have probably heard of. Originally thought to be a skin issue, it has now become evident that lupus affects many internal organs as well. Most commonly, the immune system attacks the brain, kidneys, joints, and the heart, causing pain and fatigue.

Multiple sclerosis: MS is one of the more deadly autoimmune diseases. In this case, the nervous system is attacked, and the protective myelin around the nerves is destroyed. This results in poor communication between the body and brain, which makes people feel numb and gradually lose the ability to walk and balance. It slowly robs the affected person of their ability to move and do things on their own, even affecting speech, until eventually, it affects even heart and lung function.

Psoriasis: Everyone grows new skin cells on a regular basis, and we are constantly losing or shedding old skin cells. With psoriasis, the immune system attacks the skin and causes the cells to grow far too fast. They build up in patches and become inflamed and itchy. Psoriasis can also pass to the joints and cause a form of arthritis that is very painful.

Rheumatoid arthritis: This form of autoimmune disease involves the joints. Your immune system goes after the joints, and you'll find that your joints tend to be hot, red, and stiff. It can be so painful as to affect your daily activities.

Sjögren's syndrome: In this syndrome, the glands that keep your mouth and eyes lubricated are affected. It can also attack the joints, causing inflammation there, but the most common symptoms are dry eyes and mouth.

Type 1 diabetes mellitus: Your pancreas is responsible for secreting insulin to regulate the blood sugar levels throughout the body. However, with this type of diabetes, your immune system fights against the pancreas. This destroys the cells that are responsible for making insulin and causes the patient to take insulin via injection for life.

These are just a few of the many autoimmune diseases that can affect you. They tend not to be constant but can have what is referred to as flares, where the symptoms become much worse for a period. This often coincides with high stress, sickness, or other issues that place more pressure on the body.

Signs that you have an inflammation problem, or an autoimmune disease include:

-Aches and pains

-Swelling

-Redness in specific areas

-Low-grade fever

-Fatigue

-Hair falling out

-Rashes on skin

-Tingling in the extremities

-Difficulty focusing

-Memory issues

If these symptoms persist, even after you should be over a regular cold or other illness, it's possible your immune system is attacking your body itself. The resulting inflammation could become worse and then improve, but it will likely continue to be an issue until the underlying problem is resolved.

While immune system responses that because disease are becoming more common now, it may be brought under control by using vagus nerve stimulation, which reduces inflammation.

Managing Inflammation with Vagus Nerve Stimulation

Inflammation is controlled by the vagus nerve, and when it is low in tone, you will find that there is a lot more inflammation in your body. When the nerve is stimulated, it lets the immune system know that it should calm down. The result is less chronic inflammation and better health.

Your immune system can malfunction just like everything else in the body, but when it does, it has widespread effects. Chronic inflammation will cause poor health and can even result in death if it gets bad enough. That's right, and your own body can kill you if the inflammation gets out of control. Therefore, people die from autoimmune diseases.

It's obviously best to prevent mistaken immune system responses, but the current method is to dose people up with medications that lower the immune system. These are the same drugs used to treat cancer, and they have their own side effects. It's also not a good idea to restrict your immune system for long periods of time, as this can leave you open to a lot of other diseases and will limit your lifestyle.

It's far better to aim for natural methods of reducing inflammation. Eating a healthy diet and eliminating sugar and processed foods from your diet is a good start, but frequent stimulation of the vagus nerve is also useful. It will help your body lower the inflammation and prevent the creation of more white blood cells, which can be an issue when there are too many of them.

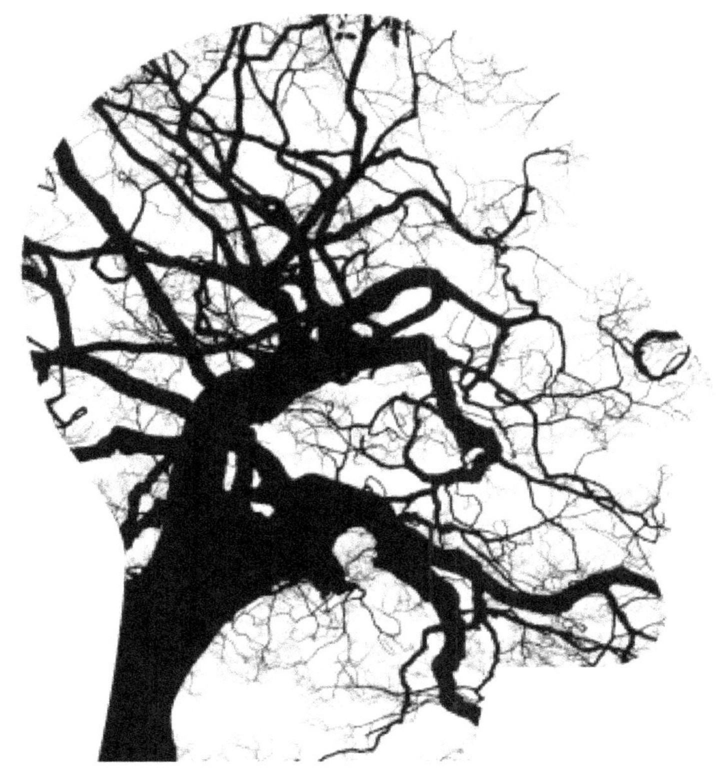

Chapter 4 The Benefits of Vagus Nerve Stimulation

The thought of going to the hospital or seeking some form of treatment usually feels us with dread. They are synonymous with pain and suffering, and while no one likes going to the doctor, we all get infections or ailments from time to time that requires medical care and treatment. However, there are ways that we can tap into the natural self-healing power of the body and reduce the number of times that we need to seek medical intervention,

Diseases are a natural part of life because our bodies are susceptible to the wear and tear that comes with age as well as infections and physical damage inflicted by pathogens and other stimuli. This means that the quest for good health is a never-ending journey because we cannot escape the inevitable effect of nature and our surroundings on our health.

Whether you find your comfort at the bottom of the pill bottle, or in alternative therapies, our goal ultimately remains the same; to improve our quality of life by staying healthy and avoiding diseases. The quest for longevity has led to the development of research in various aspects of medicine, from disease prevention, diagnosis, treatment, and cure, the winding road to better health has led to important findings that we can use to better our health.

While human advances in medicine cannot be downplayed, it is important to remember that medicine has side effects on the body. When taken for prolonged periods of time, conventional medicine can have adverse effects on our bodies in the form of side effects. While conventional medicine is beneficial for the treatment of various ailments and conditions, we should do the necessary to reduce the incidences where we need to take it and avoid over-reliance on pills and potions.

In an ideal situation, being able to stimulate the vagus nerve effectively will enable the body to become more adept at keeping illnesses at bay, meaning that you will need less medical intervention to stay healthy. The body's self-healing mechanism functions best when the internal environment is in a rested state.

This means that when the fight and flight responses are activated, the body's self-healing mechanism cannot work. Therefore, when you unleash the parasympathetic power of the vagus nerve through stimulation, you effectively shut down the fight or flight responses and activate the body's self-healing mechanisms.

The 10th cranial nerve, which is the Vagus nerve, is the longest nerve in the body extending from the brain through the neck and thorax all the way to the gut. This nerve, with its sensory and motor response functions, has significant roles in the regulation of organs such as the heart, lungs, and gut. The parasympathetic roles of the vagus nerve, which inhibit the effects of the sympathetic nervous system, meaning that the vagus nerve is an important factor for proper organ function and optimum physical and mental health.

The roles of the vagus nerve in maintaining homeostasis and balance in the internal environment of the body have led to the discovery that the vagus nerve can be used not only in boosting our overall immunity but also in facilitating the body's self-healing mechanism.

Now that we can appreciate how important the vagus nerve is when it comes to good health, the next question would be, how do you measure the activity of the vagus nerve? That is where the vagal tone comes in.

Vagal Tone

Vagal tone is the term used to refer to the activity of the vagus nerve. The activity of the vagus nerve has significant effects on:

- heart rate regulation
- vasodilation and constriction of vessels,
- glandular activity in the heart,
- glandular activity lungs
- gastrointestinal sensitivity and motility and
- regulation of inflammation.

When it comes to health, the vagal tone is measured in terms of the consistent nature of the parasympathetic action that the vagus nerve exerts. While the vagal input is constant, the degree of the stimulation it exerts is influenced by various factors including the parasympathetic responses of the autonomic nervous system. This means that the vagal tone will vary depending on the internal environment in the body. For instance, when the body is in a state of fight or flight, then the vagal tone or activity will be diminished.

Vagal tone can be used as an indicator of various organ functions in the body, including cardiac function, and may also be used in assessing emotional regulation or any other factors that can be influenced by parasympathetic responses such as digestive functions.

The measurement of vagal tone is done using either invasive or noninvasive procedures. Measurement of the vagal tone using invasive procedures is characterized by the use of manual or electrical methods to stimulate the vagus nerve. When it comes to non-invasive techniques, the vagal tone is typically determined by the assessment of the heart rate and heart rate variability. Heart rate variability (HRV) is the difference in the time lapse that occurs between heartbeats.

When the vagal tone is high, then the heart rate is typically slower, and on the other hand, an increased heart rate is an indication that vagus nerve activity is diminished. The vagal tone in the body is a useful tool in the determination of emotional, psychological, and even possible physical disorders that may manifest as a result of poor vagal activity or function.

Vagus Nerve Stimulation

The vagus nerve has both afferent and efferent functions in connecting the brains to organs such as the heart, lungs, and gut. This means that it facilitates communication from the brain to the organs (afferent) and communication to the brain from the organs (efferent).

The vagus nerve functions in controlling motor responses in the voice box, diaphragm, heart, and stomach. In addition, it has sensory functions in the ears and tongue. The widespread nature of the influence on the vagus nerve on different organs, therefore, makes it a useful treatment therapy in patients with diseases caused by chronic inflammation, including Alzheimer's, Epilepsy, and Rheumatoid arthritis.

When Vagus nerve stimulation therapy is to be used on a patient, a device that is similar to a pacemaker is implanted in the chest of the patient. A wire from this device is then run from the device to the vagus nerve in the neck by making incisions on the left side of the neck, which allows for the wire to be placed beneath the skin. This device then functions by sending electrical impulses to the vagus nerve which, in turn, transmits these signals to the brain.

These pulses that are transmitted to the brain are used in the treatment of patients with conditions such as drug-resistant depression. The impulses help in battling depression by affecting the circuits in the limbic system of the brain, which is the area that is responsible for our moods and emotions.

In epilepsy, vagus nerve stimulation therapy works in a similar manner. The signals transmitted from the implanted device travel to the vagus nerve, where they are then sent on to the brain. These mild electrical pulses sent to the brain help in controlling the abnormal brain activity that causes epileptic seizures. While vagus nerve stimulation therapy does not cure epilepsy, it plays a big role in reducing the frequency, duration, and severity of epileptic seizures. This therapy has become an important tool in the management of epilepsy.

Perhaps one of the most incapacitating illness, that is caused by chronic inflammation in the joints is rheumatoid arthritis. Not only does it result in severe joint pain, but rheumatoid arthritis also restricts movement as well, and may lead to joint deformities in the long run. This disease is challenging for patients because it severely affects the quality of life by limiting the independence of the sufferer. It has no cure meaning that the patient needs to learn to limit and slow down the degeneration in the joints.

Vagus nerve stimulation therapy has proven to be useful in the management of the inflammation that causes joint degradation, and as such, helping in slowing down the course of rheumatoid arthritis and minimizing symptoms such as joint pain and swelling. When the vagus nerve is activated, it releases acetylcholine and inhibits the production of the tumor necrosis factor from the pancreas.

Both of these mechanisms initiated by the vagus nerve are effective in the reduction of inflammation, and therefore, offer relief in terms of the level of inflammation in terms of swelling, pain, and deformation of the joints. In rheumatoid arthritis, vagus nerve stimulation therapy can be invasive, as in the case of surgically implanting a device to function as a pacemaker or non-invasive where the vagus nerve is stimulated externally.

Vagus nerve stimulation therapy has been used in the treatment of patients with gastroparesis. Gastroparesis is the condition where food movement through the gut is inhibited, resulting in food staying in the stomach too long and blockages being formed. This disease can lead to bacterial infections, abdominal pain, bloating, loss of appetite, and weight loss. Vagus nerve therapy functions by innervating the muscles in the digestive tract that facilitate the movement of food in the digestive system through peristalsis.

These are all classic examples of situations where vagus nerve therapy is used in conjunction with conventional medical intervention to realize quicker treatment or aid in alleviating symptoms that do not necessarily respond to medical pills. However, vagus nerve activation is not only useful for people who are already sick. This nerve can help you in maintaining and improving your physical health and mental state, and as such, we can all benefit from the self-healing powers of this powerful nerve that makes up part of the body's self-healing mechanism.

Cardiovascular Health

The vagus nerve functions in the control of our heart rate, in effect, acting as a natural pacemaker. By stimulating heart muscles, it can effectively slow down our heart rate when it is too fast as happens in stressful conditions.

When the heart rate is increased, it can lead to elevation of the blood pressure, which causes strain on the heart tissue and blood vessels.

By lowering the heart rate, the vagus nerve effectively reduces blood pressure, and by extension, reduces the pressure on the cardiac muscles. A properly functioning vagus nerve is, therefore, crucial for cardiovascular health and in avoiding conditions such as hypertension.

When out tissues get infected, the body responds to the attack by activating the immune system, which dispatches white blood cells to the scene of infection to neutralize the threat. These responses result in inflammation, which is characteristic in cases of physical injury or illness.

However, when an inflammatory response triggered by the immune system is prolonged, it causes the body to start attacking its own cells resulting in chronic inflammation. Chronic inflammation leads to autoimmune conditions such as rheumatoid arthritis.

The vagus nerve is able to effectively control inflammation by inhibiting the overstimulation of the immune system that is caused by the sympathetic nervous system. Medical research has shown that stimulation of the vagus nerve helps in resolving conditions related to prolonged inflammation of tissues in the body.

Breathing

Our ability to breathe is controlled by our lungs, which are regulated by the Vagus nerve through the neurotransmitter acetylcholine. Proper breathing is not only an effective way to deal with pain but is also effective in coping with stress by creating a calming effect on the body.

Relaxation techniques such as meditation and yoga incorporate breathing techniques because proper breathing has a relaxing effect on the body.

Improved Memory

Stimulation of the vagus nerve has been found to have an effect on improving memory. This is accomplished through the neurotransmitter norepinephrine being released into the amygdala, which forms part of the limbic system. This means that the activation of the vagus nerve can be beneficial in counteracting the effects of some cognitive disorders.

Weight Management

Communication in the gut-brain axis is facilitated by the vagus nerve. When the vagus nerve function is impaired, it loses the sensitivity that enables it to detect fullness in the stomach. When the vagus nerve cannot send a message to the brain that the stomach is full, it means you will not be able to know when you are full or not, and this is likely to cause overeating.

Stimulating the vagus nerve increases its sensitivity to the fullness signal from the stomach, and this increased sensitivity will cause you to feel fuller faster and, as such, will result in reduced food intake.

Stress Management

When the body's sympathetic responses have been activated, we go into flight and fight mode. One of the characteristics of being in fight or flight mode is the release of the stress hormone cortisol. Cortisol is a stress hormone released by the adrenal glands. The sympathetic system triggers the release of cortisol in response to various stress factors.

However, when cortisol levels remain elevated for prolonged periods of time, it has a myriad of harmful effects, including weight gain, high blood pressure, insomnia, and chronic fatigue. The vagus nerve, with its parasympathetic effects of inhibiting sympathetic responses, can effectively inhibit the release of cortisol by putting your body back into a rested and relaxed state. It is for this reason that people with a stronger vagus nerve response recover faster from illness or stress.

Gut Feelings

Have you ever been walking on a dark street and felt the hairs on the back of your neck stand up? Or just met a person and had an instinctive response that you could not really explain? Well, that is called a gut feeling, and though many of us regard them as fancies or whims, gut feelings are actually very real. The gut is capable of conveying your feelings to the brain through the vagus nerve in the form of electrical impulses. This communication facilitated by the vagus nerve through the gut-brain axis is vital to our mental health as it impacts how we behave.

Chapter 5 Understanding PTSD, Trauma

Trauma is something everyone experiences at some point in their lives. While it can be overcome, trauma can have a long-lasting impact on an individual, causing distress diminishing self-worth, and causing a wide range of psychological concerns. On top of the psychological effects, trauma can greatly impair an individual's physical health due to its side effects.

Trauma occurs as a natural response from the body trying to cope and manage overwhelming, disturbing, and stressful situations or events. Trauma can cause an individual to feel hopeless, depressed, and significant distrust. Traumatic events can occur for multiple reasons such as:

- Natural disasters

- War

- Loss of control over oneself

- Betrayal

- Abuse (physical, verbal, or emotional)

- Events that cause an individual to question their abilities

- Accidents

- Medical conditions

- Physical pain

- Personal assault or non-personal assault.

Types Of Trauma

Trauma is often classified under two categories, small t traumas, and large T traumas. The trauma an individual experience is solely based on the way they perceived the situation and the effect it has on them. The two categories of trauma are simply set up as a guideline to determine the level of trauma one has experienced.

Small "t" Trauma

These types of trauma do not comprise of physical threats to the individual and their life is typically not in imminent danger. Small "t" traumas are often disregarded are rarely addressed. They can include:

- Financial strain

- Work stress

- Starting a new job

- Relationship conflicts

- Legal troubles.

Many life changes can fall into the small "t" trauma category. When unaddressed, however, these types of trauma can follow an individual for their lifetime and unknowing cause additional issues. When trauma is left unprocessed or ignored, these small "t" traumas can cause a build-up of anxiety and stress. Most of these traumas are usually easy to overcome and move on from.

Large "T" Trauma

These types of trauma are more challenging to deal with and they bring about an insurmountable amount of distress and feelings of helplessness. Many times, these events will only occur once in a lifetime; others can be prolonged events that lead an individual seeing no end of the distress in sight. Large "T" trauma is not easily ignored but many individuals try to avoid them at all costs. Types of large "T" trauma can include:

- Emotional abuse

- Verbal abuse

- Physical abuse

- Sexual abuse

- Child abuse

- Neglect

- Natural disasters.

Large "T" traumas can carry several triggers that remind the individual of the event. While people who experience this try to avoid thinking about these triggers. Avoidance typically leads to more severe reactions. For an individual to fully move on from a large "T" trauma, they need to first properly heal from the pain and distress it has caused. While this is not easily or quickly accomplished, it is necessary for them to return to a more normal way of life.

Acute Stress Disorder

Mild trauma can lead to acute stress disorder. This can cause a person to have a variety of traumatic symptoms, but they tend to only last for a few weeks and can slowly go away on their own.

Trauma can cause mental, physical, and psychological symptoms, which can include:

- Sadness

- Fear

- Shame

- Anger

- Nausea

- Dizziness

- Sleep disturbances

- Headaches

- Digestive issues

- Loss of appetite

- Insomnia

- Irregular emotional control

- Anxiety

- Addiction

- Depression.

When trauma is left untreated or not appropriately processed, these conditions can worsen and become debilitating. The side effect can lead to more severe health problems.

PTSD can arise out of traumatic occurrences. Those with PTSD tend to have symptoms of trauma and/or acute stress disorder but the symptoms never diminish and can last for months or longer. The longer the symptoms are present, the more debilitating and severe they become. This type of trauma is often the result of a person being directly or indirectly affected by a physical attack. The traumatic events cause the individual to ruminate over the experience. Disturbing thoughts, feelings, and flashbacks haunt the individual and these can remain present for months and years after the traumatic event has happened.

Those with PTSD have a negative reaction to anything that reminds them of the trauma. They can act out aggressively and abusively exhibit behavior that can be viewed as detached or erratic. The symptoms tend to be grouped into four categories, but the severity of the symptoms can range greatly. These symptom categories include:

1. Intrusive thoughts

These symptoms include memories, dreams, and flashbacks that occur involuntarily. Each of these can be incredibly realistic to the individual suffering from PTSD that they can often mistake their flashbacks or daydreams as actually occurring in real time. These symptoms affect the individual significantly as they cause the person to unwilling relive the event repeatedly.

2. Avoidance

When individuals face such intense traumatic events, it is not uncommon for them to want to avoid talking or thinking about the events. Those with PTSD go out of their way to avoid remembering any details about the event. They will often make a point to avoid people, places, situations, objects, or activities that can remind them of what they experienced. This avoidance carries over to avoiding how they feel about the events.

3. Negative thoughts or feelings

Negative thoughts of those with PTSD go far beyond the usual negative self-talk that most participate in. Those with PTSD have a constant loop of negativity whirling in their heads, both about how they feel about themselves and about those around them. PTSD can cause a person to lose trust in their closest friends and family and they may even feel these individuals may cause them harm or are out to get them. This causes individuals to immediately lose interest in the things they used to enjoy doing. They are often overcome with feelings of shame, guilt, fear, and rage and that makes it impossible for them to participate in activities they once enjoyed.

4. Reaction symptoms

Reaction symptoms are those the individual exhibit when reminded of the traumatic event. These symptoms can cause an individual to become reckless, self-destructive, easily irritated to the point that they verbally or physically lash out at things around them, unable to sleep or concentrate, and may find ways to "self-medicate" such as drinking excessively.

How Does This Impact Daily Life?

The symptoms, no matter how mild, can have significant impairments on an individual's life. When individuals hold on to past events, this has a direct impact on the autonomic nervous system. These traumas affect how we speak, how we move, how we express ourselves, and how we hold ourselves or our posture. Individuals who suffer from PTSD live impaired lives and often lack the mental, physical, and emotional capacity to function day-to-day.

PTSD can cause the manifestation of:

- Intense pain

- Digestive issues

- Hormonal imbalance

- Disruption to the immune system

- Depression

- Addiction.

How Does the Vagus Nerve Impact Trauma?

When individuals are faced with constant trauma, they are unable to allow the parasympathetic nervous system to become active and the vagus nerve reduces the fight or flight response. They often enter a state of constant shutdown where they feel they are not living their own life. This leads to confusion and the inability to recognize a safe situation, places, or people. Those who suffer from PTSD can suffer more severely from this as they are more likely to replay the traumatic events repeating through their minds. When they continuously loop these memories, it makes it more difficult for them to distinguish between what is real and what is just a recollection of past events. For individuals to learn to cope with their trauma, they need to be able to break this negative loop.

Breathing plays a major part in overcoming trauma. Those with PTSD frequently suffer from panic or anxiety attacks. This causes their breathing to be rapid and focused in the upper chest. Breathing in this manner is linked to the sympathetic nervous system and can trigger the shutdown response. This type of response to fear and trauma is associated with primitive survival skills. When you see an animal face a predator, they will often freeze and/or play dead. This is a defense mechanism they have developed to get predators to walk by instead having them for lunch. While this is effective for in the wild when facing down a lion, for humans this response is a hindrance and not the way many want to live out their days. Being able to notice and regain control over your breathing can help the vagus nerve and parasympathetic system click on. Unfortunately, this is easier said than done for those who must face the traumatic memories.

While it can take a great deal of practice being able to put a sudden stop to the shutdown response, gaining control of your breathing and working through your trauma instead of avoiding it can be done. With vagus nerve stimulation and toning, individuals can retrain their systems to react in a more appropriate manner when facing trauma. Even those with severe PTSD can benefit from learning how to perform quick vagus nerve activation techniques to help work through traumatic episodes. Through vagus nerve stimulation, those suffering through trauma and/or PTSD can rewire their process and become unstuck from the fight or flight, or shutdown, phases.

Vagus Nerve Exercises That Can Help Individuals Overcome Ptsd And Trauma

The methods described here can be used at any time, any place. Some of these allow you to quickly stimulate the vagus nerve in order to better manage your stress and anxiety. Others will need to regularly practice this in order to obtain the most benefits. Those with PTSD should consider adding these techniques and methods with additional talk and/or cognitive therapy. When used with traditional forms of therapy, one can fully learn how to address, process, and heal from their trauma.

Ways to Quickly Snap Out of the Shutdown Response Through Vagus Nerve Activation

There are three main ways in which a person can quickly snap out of the shutdown response and activate their vagus nerve:

1. Splash cold water on your face to slow the heart rate and lower the body pressure.

2. Take in a deep breath, hold it for a few seconds, and then slowly exhale through the nose; repeat three to five times.

3. Chant a simple positive mantra such as "I am safe" or "I am strong."

Vagus Nerve Stimulation to Heal from PTSD

Stimulating the vagus to stop the sympathetic system is done when the individuals feels safe and secure. The following activities can instantly promote varying levels of these feelings.

1. Make connections with others. Though challenging to feel as if you can trust others, the best way to switch from the sympathetic

nervous system to the parasympathetic nervous system is to make a connection with someone else.

2. Hug. Along with the first technique, hugging helps us feel safe and connected to others. By giving or receiving a hug, you can instantly trigger the vagus nerve.

3. Laugh. If hugging is not really your thing, you can laugh instead. Laughing can help stimulate the vagus nerve to release oxytocin. Oxytocin encourages you to make connections with others and lift your mood. Laughing, just like hugging, helps you feel connected with others and can strengthen bonds.

4. Shake it off. One of the ways you can bounce out of the shutdown mode is to do a full body shake. Before you go into a full out shake, do a quick body scan. Are there any areas of your body that feel tense or stiff? If you find tension in your body, these are the areas you want to focus on when you wiggle and shake. Give each area your attention as you shake the tension out. When you have gone through all the areas and feel relieved, pause for a moment to take in the stillness that surrounds you and let it fill you. This is your body waking up again. This is the feeling you want to recall when facing a trauma-induced memory or episode.

Daily Long-Term Vagal Toning Technique for Trauma and PTSD

Healing from trauma or PTSD can be a life-long process. Strengthening the vagus nerve daily results in developing the skills necessary for your mind and body to bounce back from traumatic events and experiences that trigger trauma symptoms. The following daily exercises you can perform to receive long-term benefits from the vagus nerve:

1. Bhramari pranayama. The Bhramari pranayama is referred to as the humming bee breath in yoga practice. This type of breath work helps you tone the vagus nerve by stimulating it through the vocal cords. When you perform this breath, you can keep the nervous system calm and prevent it from going into fight or flight mode. To perform this type of breathwork, get into a comfortable sitting position on the floor or on your bed. Cross your legs and bring your hands to cover yours ears. Your thumbs should face down towards the ground. Take a deep breath in; as you exhale, begin to make a humming sound that vibrates through your ears. You can repeat this process as many times as you need.

2. Sleep on your right side. Trauma and PTSD have severe negative effects on sleep, and how you sleep can add to these difficulties. Sleeping on the right side of your body can stimulate the vagus nerve and lead to a more restful night's sleep. You should avoid sleeping on your back as this is often the worst position for vagus nerve stimulation.

3. Tai chi or qigong. Like yoga, tai chi and qigong are forms of slow movement exercises that stimulate and tone the vagus nerve. These practices focus on strengthening the internal systems through precise moment and breath. Sun Style tai chi is a type of tai chi the utilize smooth, flowing movements that can help individuals feel grounded. This is an important aspect for those with PTSD as they can often feel lost and unsure of where they are, which results in panic, frustration, and confusion. Doing a simple Sun Style tai chi sequence can tone the vagus nerve and be an effective way to help heal from trauma.

Chapter 6 Vagus Nerve and Anxiety Disorder

A normal day of an individual is always filled with several activities and situations. These activities can make an individual be anxious. It is a normal phenomenon for an individual to be anxious in his life. However, there are people who develop anxiety disorders over a period. Anxiety disorders are always associated with persistent, intense and excessive for of fear and worry about the situations and activities the daily of a human being is characterized with.

 These feelings of anxiety are very detrimental. They have the potential of affecting an individual's day to day life. It makes it difficult for an individual to be in control of his or her day because of anxiety. It becomes even difficult since experiencing anxiety disorders goes to making a person's life to be in danger. It is because the mind perceives normal things largely out of proportion. An individual characterized by anxiety disorder is prone to avoiding the life situations that make him or her be anxious.

History Of Anxiety Disorders

 These disorders were discovered by the American Psychiatric Association in the year 1980. There was a very interesting diagnosis that used to happen before this recognition. A generic diagnosis of stress and was one which was given to people who suffered from anxiety disorders. This was because medical practitioners did not understand what entailed in anxiety disorders. In turn, very few people were able to receive effective treatment leaving most people on the loop. However, there have been several types of research that have been conducted that show how people suffer a great deal with these anxiety disorders. These suffering can be avoided if these diagnosis and treatment are done in the early stages of ailment.

There have been several awareness campaigns carried out by people over the years. However, recent years have seen a major focus by the media on the prevalence of anxiety disorders. This has made several people be aware of the general knowledge about anxiety disorders. The modern years has seen development and advancements of better and appropriate ways of treating these conditions. There are more patients from different walks of life who are getting treatment for anxiety disorders. It is because the level of stigma associated with anxiety disorders has dropped.

The early years had an intriguing thought about anxiety disorders. People associated with panic attacks and anxiety disorders as a problem faced by only women. This ideology was found to be fallacious over years of research and study from interested parties. However, it is shown by studies that men tend to be less hesitant to receive treatment. This is despite the conditions affecting both men and women. These conditions have been in existence for a very long time. It is only the recent awareness and recognition that has seen the rise in patient's numbers. Several leaders in the past have been reported to experiencing panic attacks and different forms of anxiety disorders. The form of treatments offered in the past was diverse and can be termed humorous. The forms of treatment offered very ineffective to patients. There were certain moments that the forms of treatment were very dangerous to an individual. The forms of treatment in the past involved use of balms and herbs, bloodletting with the usage of leeches, application of extremely hot temperature to a patient and bathing in extremely cold rivers and lakes. This dawn was ended by the new form of psychoanalysis. One of the greatest psychologists who spearheaded the research was known as

Freud. Several people turned their ways to therapeutic solutions when faced with anxiety disorders. Several advancements have been seen over the years to the development of drugs that have proved to be very helpful to people. People with an adverse level of anxiety disorders have been prescribed these drugs for their betterment.

Types Of Anxiety Disorders

1. Panic Disorder

There are moments an individual experiences panic attacks that are consistent and unexpected. The common definition of what panic attacks are is; they are surges that appear abruptly to an individual which are filled with intense levels of fears. These panic attacks can reach their peak in a couple of few seconds. People who suffer from this condition tend to leave their life in the utmost form of fear because of the panic attacks. There are several ways that an individual can know if he or she is suffering from panic attacks. A person is likely to suffer from panic attacks if he or she feels an overwhelming sense of terror which has does not have any obvious cause for it. There are also physical symptoms that characterize panic attacks. They include racing of heart, sweating and breathing complications. A large population across the globe experience panic attacks either once or twice across their lifetime. There was a recent report that was prepared by the American Psychological Association which had a critical finding. The report stated that out of seventy-five people, one person is likely to experience or ail from panic disorder. There are several things that a person who suffers from panic attack experiences. He or she can be in fear of experiencing another form of a panic attack if this situation has happened twice in a span of one month.

The symptoms of panic disorders have been seen to be quite overwhelming by people. However, there is good news in the present world we live in. It is because these symptoms can be managed and be improved through the current form of treatment. An individual ailing from this condition is encouraged to seek medical help. The situation has the possibility of running a person's life because it is detrimental. It reduces a person's productivity and attainment of quality life because it affects a person's day to day life.

Symptoms of Panic Disorder

There is a certain age that the symptoms of panic disorder can manifest themselves clearly. It begins to manifest clears in teens and young adults who are around the ages of twenty-five years. An individual is termed to be suffering from panic disorders when the panic attacks happen more than four times. It was also sensible to be diagnosed with a panic disorder when you leave in constant fear and worry of experiencing panic attacks after suffering from one. There are no warning signings that are accompanied by panic attacks.

There is a period that occurs abruptly with intense levels of fear which lasts up to an estimated time of twenty to thirty minutes. There are also extreme cases of panic attacks that have been experienced by several people across the globe. This entails the problem of going to a level of panic attacks lasting up to more than one hour. Therefore, panic attacks tend to differ in the experiences of several people in the globe. The common symptoms include; shortness in breathing, increased in the heart palpitations, dizziness, sweating chest pains, fear, nausea, and lightheadedness.

2. Post-Traumatic Stress Disorder

Life events that are terrifying are the major cause of this disorder. These terrific life experiences can either have been experienced or have been witnessed by an individual. There are several things that go on when a person is suffering from posttraumatic stress. He or she is prone to having nightmares, severe anxiety and flashbacks. It goes a higher level to the person experiencing deep thoughts about the event that are uncontrollable. There are different life situations that can be traumatizing. These events include rape, terror attracts and accidents just to mention a few. They really affect an individual to the core since they affect an individual daily life. It takes time for an individual to adjust from these situations to cope with his normal lifestyle. However, this is not the endpoint for an individual suffering from post-traumatic stress. It is because; good health care can be able to make him or her get better. An individual is supposed to seek treatment from a reliable medical facility. A good form of treatment has the potential of reducing these effects that affect an individual's daily activities.

Symptoms of Post-Traumatic Stress Disorder

It has a different way its symptoms manifest themselves. They tend to manifest in an individual after an estimated time of one month. The one moth stated is after the occurrence of the traumatic event. The symptoms of posttraumatic events have a severe impact on an individual's life. They affect a person's life from his or her work and transcend to affecting his social relationships with family and friends. This leads to low productivity in the normal tasks that an individual is supposed to undertake.

This form of anxiety order symptoms is always grouped into four different groups. These groups include; negative change in thinking and moods, avoidance, changes in emotion and physical reaction, and intrusive memories. These situations are not like everybody who suffers from post-traumatic stress. This even makes the base of symptoms of posttraumatic stress being different from people who are diagnosed with the disorder.

Intrusive memories are characterized with; recurrent of stressful memories about the traumatic event, revealing of the traumatizing events as if they were reoccurring, dreams that seem upsetting and nightmares that relate to the traumatic event and severe emotional distress of anything that can remind an individual about the traumatizing experience. The symptoms categorized under avoidance include an individual avoid thinking about the traumatic event.

The category of changes in a person's mood and thoughts has several signs. Some of these symptoms include; having negative thoughts about oneself and the world in general, loss of hope about the future, having difficulty in memories, difficulty when it comes to maintaining close relationships with people, detachments from friends and family and feeling of being emotionally numb. The last category of symptoms is those that are grouped under changes in emotional and physical reactions. These symptoms include; being frightened easily, overwhelming levels of guilt, trouble when it comes to a person concentrating, trouble when it entails concentrating and development of self-destructing behavior.

3. SOCIAL ANXIETY DISORDER

It is very normal for an individual to feel a certain form of being nervous in certain situations life presents us with. A good depiction can be a person going for a date or making a huge presentation at work. These situations have the potential of making a person experience butterflies in his or her stomach. However, this is different in a person who is suffering from a social anxiety disorder which is also known as social phobia. The difference is portrayed when an individual suffering from this disorder is anxious and faced with overwhelming levels of fear and embracement from being judged and scrutinized.

The levels of fear and anxiety that individual experience in social anxiety disorder is detrimental. They have the potential of affecting an individual's daily life experiences. The life experiences cut across through educational, professional and social life. Learning to cope with the skills that psychotherapy helps to bring an individual to a recovery stage. There are cases where are an individual experience severe impact because of social anxiety disorder, an individual is prescribed drugs during these situations.

Symptoms of Social Anxiety Disorder

There are moments in life where an individual feel shy and discomfort in certain situations. These feelings sometimes are not characteristics of social anxiety disorder. People likely to have such experiences are children. The comfort a person is likely to experience largely depends on an individual's traits and his or her experiences in the present situation. Social anxiety starts to portray itself on teens. There are also moments or situations that it is seen in children and adults.

Symptoms of social anxiety disorder are characterized into two groups. These groups include behavioral and emotional symptoms and physical symptoms. Symptoms classified under behavioral and emotional signs include; fear of situations, worry about embarrassment, the fright of talking with strangers and fear of being noticed. On the other hand, symptoms related to physical symptoms include blushing, increased heart rate, sweating, muscle tension, dizziness and stomach upset.

Major Causes Of Anxiety Disorders

There are several factors that can lead to a person developing anxiety disorders. The normal life of an individual is characterized by the occurrence of different activities. These activities cut across his or her social, educational and professional edges just to mention few facets of life. These activities and situations have the potential of making an individual develop anxiety disorders over time. It is a very complicated topic for several peoples because human is different. Therefore, causes of anxiety tend to differ in several people.

 The cause of anxiety can be complicated sometimes. It is because it has the potential of being caused by a combination of chained issues. These issues can either be induced by the general environment an individual is accustomed to leaving in. The common causes of anxiety from the environment an individual resides in can be life experiences, emotions or certain events. It is important for a person to know the causes of anxiety disorders. It is because it has myriad advantages such as keeping an individual in shape of his daily life to reduce or avoid the causes. These causes include:

 1. Medication

Anxiety has the potential to make an individual make panic, fell restless and nervous. This happens even in a situation where an individual is not in danger. These feelings can be as a result of the medication an individual is taking because of other health conditions he or she is suffering from. There are two probable causes that these medications may bring to an individual.

They have the potential of making an individual experience these attacks for the fir first time or worsen the attacks if they were experienced earlier on. These effects by drugs are normally referred to as side effects of treatments. However, there are drugs that target a specific part of a human body that plays a critical part in anxiety. They include;

a. Medications with Caffeine

There are some medications that treat migraine and headaches that have caffeine as their component. These drugs have the potential for stimulating an individual's nervous system. This has an influence on making an individual's blood pressure and heart palpitations to increase. An individual has the possibility of being jittery, anxious and nervous during these moments. An individual who is prone to anxiety attacks has the possibility of developing a disorder in moments he or she is subjected to such drugs for long.

b. Corticosteroids

These drugs have a special way in which they work in an individual 's body. They work similarly to how hormones produced in the body conduct their functions. These drugs are used to treating certain conditions in an individual's life. They are commonly used to treat bronchitis, arthritis, asthma, and allergies. These symptoms presented in anxiety disorders are presented when an individual is presented to taking cortisone, prednisone, and dexamethasone.

c. ADHD Drugs

The medications used in these cases are always described as stimulations. This means that they have a large magnitude in affecting an individual's brain. These types of drugs have the potential to change how a person's nerve cells work because they change how they send messages from the environment. The described impacts have the potential of changing how an individual's brains work. They subject a person's brain to a mental state of being anxious and restless in moments an individual takes them in high dosages. Mood swings are a common occurrence to an individual who has such prescriptions. It can lead to an anxiety disorder if these symptoms progress for a long time. The common drugs in this group include Focalin, Adderall, and Vyvanse.

d. Asthma Medications

Some of the drugs that are used to treat asthma have the potential of altering an individual's moods. This brings about mental states such as depression and anxiety to an individual's life. Medicines that are used to open an individual's brain have the potential of making him or her experience anxiety attacks. This phenomenon can occur even if an individual did not experience anxiety attacks even if he or she did not in the past. These drugs include albuterol, salmeterol, and theophylline.

e. Thyroid Medicine

There are several things that are bound to happen to an individual when his or her body does not make adequate thyroid fluid. An individual can have low levels of concentration, gain excessive weight or lack of energy to do his or her daily duties. This condition is commonly known as hypothyroidism. The drugs used to treat this condition are commonly known for making a patient experience panic attack.

f. Seizure Drugs

The type of medication used in this is commonly known as phenytoin. It is responsible for calming the electrical activities that happen in a person's brain in the event he or she experiences seizures. There are certain situations that a doctor can prescribe these drugs to a patient who has problems in his or her heartbeats to have a regular rhythm. The drug can have severe effects by triggering anxiety attacks on an individual. These drugs have the potential of making an individual become anxious and agitated.

g. Medicine Meant for Parkinson's Disease

During treatment of this condition, doctors prescribe a combination of two drugs most of the times. These drugs are carbidopa and levodopa. The release of capsules from rotary drugs can make an individual experience anxiety attack. If symptoms that are related to anxiety disorders persist on an individual, he or she is advised to have discussions with his or her doctor about a change of medication.

Chapter 7 Vagus Nerve Association with Stress and Chronic Stress Disorder

Did you know your vagus nerve plays a part in your mental health as well? It isn't just a physical sensation, but also a mental sensation. Sure, the fatigue and exhaustion are physical, but psychiatric conditions are affected by your vagus nerve, and in this chapter, we'll highlight just what they are, and how to properly understand the connection between your vagus nerve, and your mental health.

Your vagus nerve is a nerve that is connected to not only your brain and heart but to pretty much every upper body function.

The vagal tone you experience changes over time and vagal tone is a natural biological process within the vagus nerve. When your vagal tone is high and proper, it means you're relaxing from the stressful situation and calming down.

But your vagal tone plays a part in your emotions, and how your physical health happens. If your vagal tone is higher, then your physical and mental health will be higher too.

Your vagal tone and vagal response naturally reduce stress. Stress can make you experience both positive and negative emotions. A little bit of stress is healthy, but you should always respond to it after the stressful situation by calming down, but that's not always the case. Your vagal tone changes the brain's responses, stimulates the digestion of the body, and in general helps you to relax.

Relaxing is good for the body because if you're always stressed, you'll have trouble doing many things. Too much stress isn't good for you.

Having too much stress isn't a good thing. Stress makes you depressed, anxious, and angry, and it can affect your ability to make rational decisions, whether it's in daily life, or in the long run.

It also affects your dopamine and serotonin levels, both of which are neurotransmitters that handle our mood. Your vagus nerve handles the variability of this whenever it can, and when you're relaxed, you have more dopamine, serotonin, and you'll feel better.

For many of us, stress is a healthy way to accomplish things, but with the way life can be, it can be almost too much in many cases, and vagal tone is affected when we're stressed.

When you feel stressed, depressed, or anxious, your vagal tone changes, and oftentimes, you're more focused on negative emotions, and psychiatric conditions. Epilepsy also increases when your vagus nerve isn't properly stimulated.

You can measure this in different ways by looking at the EmWave2 waves which measure your heartrate variability, which shows your vagal tone too.

Higher vagal tone means everything is working better, and it can also help to stimulate your vagus nerve. You'll notice that when your vagus nerve is properly stimulated, you also respond to situations in a more positive manner, whether it be emotional, or physiological situations. Your brain and emotions are properly connected, and it can help offset the issues that mental illness causes to happen to you.

Your vagus nerve is the connection between your digestive system, brain, and other conditions. It also controls inflammation. But, your vagus nerve also handles mental health conditions, and there are many that your vagus nerve is attributed to.

What Conditions Does A Low Vagal Tone Cause?

Low vagal tone, or otherwise known as your vagus nerve isn't properly stimulated, causes many different conditions in the body, and some of them are significant. Besides anxiety disorders and depression, it also is found in other types of conditions.

Degenerative mental health conditions, such as Alzheimer's and dementia, were found to be connected to your vagal tone. That's because, the inflammatory response in the brain isn't curbed, which causes degeneration of the nerve cells, and thereby this condition.

Migraines and other problems in the head, including tinnitus, are also attributed to your vagus nerve. When it comes to tinnitus, it's because your vagus nerve is very close to where your ear is and wraps partially around the inner parts of the ear.

But, it's more than just these conditions. Addictions, eating disorders, personality disorders, even autism spectrum conditions are oftentimes attributed to your vagus nerve. That's because the mental health effects that come about due to the physical problems this causes can play a major role in your body's' ability to handle this.

Drug and alcohol addiction oftentimes happen because of this. It's because when the vagal tone isn't fully activated, it causes the body to seek out other alternatives since it's not getting enough serotonin in the body. For addicts, the happy feeling they get when they shoot up or take drugs, helps with this and can make them feel good, but it doesn't fix the problem of the vagus nerve not being stimulated, and oftentimes, it makes the problem worse.

But it isn't just serious conditions. Poor memory, mood swings and even mood disorders, MS, OCD, and several mental diseases and mental conditions can oftentimes come about because of this. Chronic fatigue is another problem too, and we'll get to that in just a moment.

Chronic Fatigue And Your Vagus Nerve

Your vagus nerve controls how your body handles certain conditions. When it's overstimulated, your body is fighting with the sympathetic nervous system, which is always putting you on high alert. But, if you're always on high alert, it'll make you feel thirsty and fatigued all the time.

This isn't just temporary tiredness either, it's oftentimes a serious condition, where you feel fatigued no matter what you do, and no matter how hard you try, it doesn't go away. This can be attributed partially to digestive and nerve health, but it does tie in to the vagus nerve.

So yes, chronic fatigue is caused by your vagus nerve, and it can make things very hard on you. It's also due to the breathing you're doing, because many people who have trouble breathing oftentimes suffer from improper vagal tone, and that's because people don't realize how impactful this can be on the body.

Brain Injuries

Having vagal tone that isn't properly stimulated does affect your brain and how it works. When your vagus nerve isn't properly stimulated, allowing you to get that air you so desperately need, your body won't get enough oxygen. Oftentimes, this causes vagal syncope, which is fainting involuntarily.

If you're not careful, you'll faint in a location that isn't ideal, which then causes head and brain injury. Sometimes, this trauma can be so bad you can't do anything about it, and instead, you're unable to perform functions in life.

This is probably the worst it can get, but it can negatively affect the rest of your body, even your life if you're not careful.

This is usually a more serious situation, but it's still worth mentioning, because many don't take into consideration what might happen if your vagus nerve isn't stimulated properly, and the truth is, a lot can happen if it's not, so remember that.

Vagal Tone And Mental Health

Your vagal tone is part of your mental health, and a healthy vagal tone means better mental health. You can reduce inflammation, negative feelings, loneliness, even your instances of heart attacks or stroke if you're not careful.

Many people who have a higher vagal tone as part of a feedback loop between these emotions are oftentimes happier and in better physical health.

Healthy vagal tone also affects your social conditions too. You want to talk to other ore, and don't feel held back by depression and sadness when you have healthier vagal tone. You'll notice that you're much better off if you take care of your vagal tone, and you'll notice your vagal tone will improve your social interactions.

Humans are social creatures. We need to speak to others for the most part, or else loneliness sets in. we try to fill that void as much as we can, and even introverts need someone to talk to every now and then. Your vagal tone improves when discussing subjects with others, or just simply speaking in order to generate emotions.

When you're in a good mood, and your vagal tone is healthy, you'll notice that you have better human communications, and your bonds with others become more close-knit. That's because, you're taking care of your vagal tone, and are working to improve your vagus nerve stimulation.

Your vagus nerve does tell you about the "gut feelings" and the anxiety and fear you feel within the brain, and stress and depression are regulated via the vagus nerve, and your immune system plays a part as well.

When there are more cytokines in the body, you'll have better immunity, a happier body, and you're less at risk for developing mental health conditions. Cytokines also help with some types of depression, especially those with low mood, low motivation, and low energy. If you have more control over this, you'll feel better too.

What Can We Do About This?

While you can't just "turn off" mental health conditions, stimulating your vagus nerve will help with this. By properly breathing, and taking the steps to calm the body down, it can help curb anxiety disorders, and stress-related to anxiety. It will help improve your mood.

Even just working with socialization can help with stimulation your vagus nerve. Communication has been proven to help with your vagus nerve, a properly stimulating it via communication will aid you in bettering your vagus nerve.

Chapter 8 Body and Mind Connection

People who have great enthusiastic wellbeing know about their musings, sentiments, and practices. They have learned healthy approaches to adapt to the pressure and issues that are atypical piece of life. They like themselves and have sound connections.

In any case, numerous things that occur in your life can disturb your passionate wellbeing. These can prompt healthy sentiments of pity, stress, or tension. Indeed, even great or needed changes can be as upsetting as undesirable changes. These things include:

- Being laid off from your activity

- Having a kid leave or get back

- Dealing with the demise of a friend or family member

- Getting separated or wedded

- Suffering a disease or damage

- Getting occupation advancement

- Experiencing cash issues

- Moving to another home

- Having or embracing a child.

Your body reacts to the way you think, feel, and act. This is one sort of "mind/body connection." When you are focused on, on edge, or upset, your body responds in a way that may reveal to you that something isn't right.

For instance, you may grow hypertension or a stomach ulcer after an, especially distressing occasion, for example, the passing of a friend or family member.

Way to Improved Health

There are ways that you can improve your passionate wellbeing. Initially, attempt to perceive your feelings and comprehend why you are having them. Sifting through the reasons for bitterness, stress, and uneasiness in your life can assist you with dealing with your passionate wellbeing. The following are some other supportive tips.

Discover some stunning realities about the mind-body connection:

We have the Mind-Body Connection

Regardless of whether intentionally mindful of it or not, every one of us encounters the mind-body connection regularly of our lives. Rather than thinking about the connection as something out of sight reach, or something just realistic through long stretches of yoga and reflection, recollect it is constantly here. Mouth-watering over a tasty looking sweet, or anxious "butterflies" in the stomach before making an introduction, or running a race, are overall ideal instances of characteristic personality body connections, which a large portion of us have encountered eventually. Occasionally, the mind-body connection can deliver negative results, such as neglecting to meet athletic, scholastic, or expert objectives because of dread made by the brain.

Our Bodies React to How We Think

All that we are emerges with our contemplations. With our musings, we make the world.

Buddha

As such, on the off chance that we are continually thinking negative, reckless considerations, our bodies will go with the same pattern. Enthusiastic and mental lopsidedness can begin as something like pressure incited cerebral pains, tight shoulders, and an irritated upper back, and lead to unfortunate weight increase or misfortune, a sleeping disorder, and hypertension. Then again, we can put forth a cognizant attempt to think more decidedly and to create healthy ways of dealing with stress forever's pressure and preliminaries. After some time, the condition of our passionate and psychological well-being can be harmed or help the body's resistant framework.

We Can Make Ourselves Sick & We Can Make Ourselves Well

Studies show our ways of dealing with stress and ways we handle pressure straightforwardly associate to how we manage genuine ailments, including malignant growth. Ceaseless pressure influences the body in a negative manner, and over significant stretches of time, long haul pressure can make us increasingly vulnerable to diabetes, hypertension, heart illnesses, and a few diseases.

Notwithstanding, by utilizing our intrinsic personality body connection in a constructive manner, by keeping our brains and bodies fit as a fiddle with exercise and nourishment, we can keep feelings of anxiety lower. At the end of the day, the better we can adapt by remaining quiet and decreasing mental pressure, we will thusly lessen physical worry, alongside the possibility of building up a sickness.

We Also Have a BODY-Mind Connection

If we focus, it is anything but difficult to see the effect the body has on our perspective also. For instance, when ladies' bodies are getting ready for monthly cycle, it is the hormones inside the body causing the entirety of the feared indications (cramps, swelling, weakness, enthusiastic awkwardness, and so forth.). Another case of body-mind responses is this season's cold virus. More than likely, an individual begins to feel unwell intellectually the day or a couple of days before the body uncovered the irritated throat, nasal clog, and other basic physical manifestations.

On the other side, the body-mind connection is inconceivably positive, regardless of whether it is endorphins created after exercise or stress alleviation during a back rub. In the physical stances of yoga, it is imagined that specific stances produce certain psychological states. Backbends, for instance, are thought to animate the psyche, while reversals may expedite a calmer state. Exercise can be a modest method to help our center, states of mind, and by and large wellbeing.

Nourishment Affects Both Our Bodies and Minds

It returns to that familiar adage, "We are what we eat." Every single piece or fluid going through our lips has a type of impact on our minds. Our wholesome admission, consistently, can have immense effects both negative and positive on how we feel, on account of the substance serotonin. Basically, when serotonin levels are high, we're more joyful, and when they're low, we become discouraged.

Eating such many carbs and sugar can diminish affectability to serotonin, which prompts awful states of mind, and in the long run stoutness. To adjust serotonin levels, eating protein can be the arrangement, particularly before carb admission. Rather than gobbling a sugary jolt of energy noontime, go for a nibble high in protein to keep the temperament positive and vitality up, maintaining a strategic distance from an accident later.

Standard Sleep Is a Must for Mind & Body

Besides nourishment and exercise, rest likewise assumes a tremendous job in keeping up sound serotonin levels and keeping our brains and bodies content with one another. Serotonin's essential activity in the body is to quiet, along these lines, it is intently attached to how vitality is - or isn't- used (for example exercise and rest). Without rest, our cerebrums can be contrarily influenced, by disturbing our mind's reaction to serotonin. At the end of the day, it is essential to keep up a predictable resting design, to keep the psyche and body healthy.

Reflection Can Help Our Hearts

As indicated by the American Heart Connection, medicinal proof uncovers a certifiable complementary connection between the brain and body. Practices like reflection and other unwinding strategies have appeared to change mind-body yet in addition mind-heart connections. While there is a shortage of concentrates legitimately tending to how mind-heart intercessions can help patients with the congestive cardiovascular breakdown, the AHA closed reflection could help with tension and wretchedness, which regularly match with the genuine disease.

Pondering for around 15 minutes every day can likewise help any individual who needs to remain focused and quiet for the duration of the day. Activities like reflection can help move mental observations and responses to circumstances. By getting mindful of strain and uneasiness, and interfacing with the breath, the mind will unwind, and the body will as well. In any event, removing a couple of seconds from an upsetting day to inhale unobtrusively can have comparative impacts.

Basically, we are what we think, eat, drink, say and relax. Creating and applying care to these parts of life can assist us with maintaining blissful personality body connections. Tell us how you use your mind-body connection with remain sound.

Express your sentiments in proper manners

If sentiments of stress, trouble, or tension are causing physical issues, keeping these emotions inside can aggravate you feel. It's alright to tell your friends and family when something is annoying you. In any case, remember that your loved ones may not generally have the option to assist you with managing your emotions fittingly. On these occasions, approach somebody outside the circumstance for help. Take a stab at asking your family specialist, an instructor, or a strict consultant for guidance and backing to assist you with improving your enthusiastic wellbeing.

Carry on with a healthy lifestyle

Concentrate on the things that you are appreciative of in your life. Do whatever it takes not to fixate on the issues at work, school, or home that lead to negative sentiments. This doesn't mean you need to profess to be cheerful when you feel focused on, on edge, or upset. It's critical to manage these negative emotions, however, attempt to concentrate on the positive things throughout your life, as well. You might need to utilize a diary to monitor things that cause you to feel cheerful or serene. Some exploration has indicated that having an inspirational standpoint can improve your personal satisfaction and give your wellbeing a lift. You may likewise need to discover approaches to relinquish a few things throughout your life that cause you to feel pushed and overpowered. Set aside a few minutes for things you appreciate.

Create strength

Individuals with strength can adapt to worry in a healthy manner. Versatility can be learned and fortified with various methodologies. These incorporate having social help, keeping a positive perspective on yourself, tolerating change, and keeping things in context. An instructor or advisor can assist you with accomplishing this objective with intellectual conduct treatment (CBT). Inquire as to whether this is a smart thought for you.

Quiet your psyche and body

Unwinding techniques, for example, contemplation, tuning in to music, tuning in to guided symbolism tracks, yoga, and Tai Chi are valuable approaches to bring your feelings into balance.

Reflection is a type of guided idea. It can take numerous structures. For instance, you may do it by working out, extending, or breathing profoundly. Approach your family specialist for guidance about unwinding techniques.

Deal with yourself.

To have great passionate wellbeing, it's imperative to deal with your body by having a standard daily schedule for eating well suppers, getting enough rest, and practicing assuaging repressed pressure. Abstain from indulging and don't mishandle medications or liquor, utilizing medications or liquor worthwhile motivations different issues, for example, family and medical issues.

Interesting points

Poor passionate wellbeing can debilitate your body's insusceptible framework. This makes you bound to get colds and different diseases during genuinely troublesome occasions. Additionally, when you are feeling focused on, on edge, or upset, you may not deal with your wellbeing just as you should. You may not want to work out, eating nutritious nourishments, or taking a prescription that your primary care physician endorses. You may mishandle liquor, tobacco, or different medications. Different indications of poor passionate wellbeing include:

- Back torment

- Change in craving

- Chest torment

- Constipation or looseness of the bowels

- Dry mouth

- Extreme tiredness

- General a throbbing painfulness

- Headaches

- High pulse

- Insomnia (inconvenience dozing)

- Lightheadedness

- Palpitations (the inclination that your heart is dashing)

- Sexual issues

- Shortness of breath

- Stiff neck

- Sweating

- Upset stomach

- Weight addition or misfortune

For what reason does my primary care physician need to think about my feelings?

You may not be accustomed to conversing with your primary care physician about your sentiments or issues in your own life. In any case, recollect that the individual in question can't generally tell that you're feeling focused on, on edge, or upset just by taking a gander at you. It's imperative to be straightforward with your primary care physician on the off chance that you are having these sentiments.

In the first place, the person in question should ensure that other medical issues aren't causing your physical side effects. If your side effects aren't brought about by other medical issues, you and your PCP can address the enthusiastic reasons for your manifestations. Your primary care physician may propose approaches to treat your physical manifestations while you cooperate to improve your passionate wellbeing.

Chapter 9 The Natural Healing Power of your Body with Self-Help Exercises and Techniques

Exercise

Exercise is a necessary part of healing from chronic pain. You don't have to become an active bodybuilder or an athlete, but some degree of body movement is highly desirable to prevent chronic pain. Body movements release the "stuck" energy in our body and ensure a smooth flow of energy to prevent any pain.

Exercising is a great way to reduce your anxiety. Whether you wake up earlier in the morning before you must go to work and go for a run, or if you can go when you get home from and jog around the block.

Also, if you do exercise more this will help with your self-esteem. Exercising will make you healthier and you will feel better about yourself. If you are worried about your health and it is making your anxiety worse, get out there and do some exercises. You don't even have to leave your house; you could just find an exercise DVD and start doing some exercise from your own living room. To really help lower anxiety, it is a good idea that each time you exercise to be sure it is for 30 minutes or more. Studies have shown that it takes about thirty minutes for your anxiety to lower when exercising.

If you don't want to exercise alone, grab a friend to do this activity with you. This will make you happy and you can have someone to talk to about the things you are anxious about. It's great to have someone who you can let all your feelings be expressed to who can help you. Healthy exercise has some surprising implications for those with anxiety disorders and other psychological conditions including depression. The mechanisms by which exercise, and mental health are related are not fully understood, but many medical experts around the world now acknowledge that exercise has a major impact on a wide range of psychological conditions. It is even now believed that exercise can be as effective at combating depression as many commonly prescribed drugs.

Short bursts of activity a few times a day are the type of exercise that experts recommend. A brisk walk lasting only ten minutes is believed to be enough to raise your emotional state for a couple of hours. For those with anxiety disorders, it can be hard to get out and about on occasion. For some, with severe conditions, it can seem impossible. Exercise, however, will really help to improve your emotional state and take your mind off anxiety. Use the following tips to increase your chances of successfully incorporating exercise into your life.

Moderate level intensity exercise is recommended as perfect for improving your physical health and your mental health. This includes; walking briskly, cycling, jogging or swimming. Walking and jogging should not need any investment and if you're uncomfortable alone, partner up with a friend or relative. Ideally buddy up with someone who is addressing the same issues or has a good understanding of them, for extra support.

When we exercise, the brain releases endorphins, or "feel good" chemicals that are responsible for the "high" that many people feel during and after exercise. Another benefit of exercise for those with depression is that it lends purpose and structure to each day. Outdoor exercise has been shown to be especially effective for lifting mood.

Regular exercise can help maintain a healthy weight, which can be a problem in depressed people. Exercise promotes overall wellbeing, including heart health and a toned, more muscular body. The weight-bearing aspects of exercise prevent the body from losing bone mass and decrease the risk of osteoporosis, a particular benefit for women.

People who suffer from anxiety may not be interested in exercise. When someone is overwhelmed by the stress of everyday life, working out seems less than appealing. However, research shows that exercise plays an important role in reducing anxiety symptoms.

While exercise has been clinically proven to reduce anxiety and improve mood, it can also treat several other health problems. Health issues can be a major anxiety trigger and easing the symptoms of those ailments can reduce anxiety symptoms further.

In addition, exercising can help people relax. When a person exercises, their body releases hormones that produce a calming effect. Exercise also increases body temperature, which can be very relaxing. Working up a sweat is tiring, but it's a great way to calm down.

Speed Walking

Speed walking, more often referred to as power walking or race walking, is a technique of walking at a rapid pace. Walking is a great alternative to running and is oftentimes much easier and more accessible to a greater variety of people. Walking provides all the aerobic benefits of running while steering clear of many of the injuries associated with high-impact techniques of running. The activity of walking at an increased rate then walking "normally" can help participants lose weight, tone their muscles, and increase their mood.

Not only is speed walking valuable for the muscles and joints, but it also reinforces overall health.

Stretching

Stretching is something everyone should do on a regular basis, and those with chronic back pain will benefit most from stretching the soft the muscles, ligaments, and tendons in and around the spine.

It is a fact that when motion is limited the back becomes stiff, which can result in more pain. Those who suffer from chronic back pain need to stretch regularly and perform appropriate stretching movements to benefit from the sustained and long-term relief from the increased motion.

One top recommendation for dealing with chronic pain is by getting regular exercise. Exercise will help with different types of pain - from helping with arthritis by getting your body moving, to boosting your mood, when you have pain from Crohn's disease or fibromyalgia.

Yoga can be defined as a practice based on harmonizing the mind, body, and soul. By practicing Yoga every day, you will not only explore your true self or your inner self, but also develop the feeling that you are one with nature and environment. Yoga aids the overall well-being of the body and focuses mainly on developing relationship with the natural world around us.

Pain is not just influenced by physical injury or illness, it is also greatly affected by our thoughts, anxiety, trauma, stress and emotions. Stress and pain are closely interrelated - you may experience pain when stressed and stress can also increase the intensity of the pain. When there is increased stress, your breathing becomes heavier, erratic and ragged. Your mood is also altered along with some tension and tightening of the muscles. These symptoms of chronic pain can even increase the toxins in the body and decrease oxygen levels.

 Yoga addresses these problems effectively, as it involves the techniques of deep breathing and meditation, which helps in the absorption of much-needed oxygen and in the relaxation of mind and body. These breathing techniques ensure that the muscles of the lungs, diaphragm, back, and abdomen are fully utilized. When the muscles are loose and relaxed, they can help in releasing the built-up tension in the body and facilitate proper flow of energy throughout. Stress and anxiety levels will also be reduced gradually.

Yoga, or simple stretching, are simple practices that should be applied to everyday life to reduce the tension of stress and keep the muscles in proper working order. There are specific stretches that can focus on problem areas such as the neck or lower back. These stretches can be assigned from a personal trainer, massage therapist, or physiotherapist. Yoga can be enjoyed at home or in a studio with several other participants. There are many forms of yoga ranging from hatha yoga to hot yoga. The focus in yoga is on breath control, meditation, stretching, and balance. Not all forms of yoga are spiritual with chants and mantras, if you don't feel comfortable with that form of practice.

Exercise in general is good for chronic pain, but specific exercises, especially certain yoga positions, help to decrease some types of pain, like shoulder or neck pain.

Additionally, the relaxation techniques you will learn, can teach you how to manage the different types of chronic pain more effectively.

If you are considering trying yoga techniques for your chronic pain, you need to consider the style of yoga you will do.

While all forms of yoga can be beneficial for your body, mind and spirit, certain exercises are directed towards people who are struggling with chronic pain.

There are multiple yoga poses or asanas and different stance can be used. Individuals with chronic pain should begin with a slow-paced, gentle yoga pose. Benefits of yoga include improved ability to handle stress, feeling more relaxed throughout the day and improvements in sleep quality. Studies have proven that yoga is helpful to prevent fibromyalgia, among other chronic pain conditions.

Massage therapy has become overwhelmingly popular, and rightfully so; in addition to feeling good, it has several health benefits. Massage therapy is wonderful for any type of pain, be it chronic, acute or simply from fatigue, work, and tension. There are various massage therapies available to meet all types of needs, including Shiatsu, Swedish, hot oil and deep tissue.

Massage has also been used as a natural anxiety remedy for ages; it may be as simple as rubbing your neck gently but whichever the case you are massaging it is an effective way to calm your nerves. The benefits of any massage therapy are many, including stress relief, relaxation, lowered blood pressure, lowered tension in the muscles, and it also improves deeper breathing. As the book unfolds, I will discuss therapeutic massage as a natural remedy for anxiety disorders, in this case it will be a deep and precise tool.

A skilled and trained massage therapist will know exactly what to do once the pain problem is explained. Massage also does wonders for fatigue and stress, both of which are known to increase pain and go hand in hand with arthritis and other chronic pain conditions. It can also help to calm anxiety, which often afflicts those who suffer from chronic pain.

If you can afford it, get a massage regularly - weekly or even twice per week. Physical therapists and chiropractors also offer therapeutic massage, so it may be covered under medical insurance.

There are also electronic massagers on the market that are great options. These include mobile units, which are spot massage products that target the neck or specific areas. There are also strap onto chair units that offer shiatsu for the entire back, many come with a heat option.

The most significant health benefit of massage is that it provides the sensation of touch, which is critical in both early childhood development and overall adult health. Levels of somatotropin, or human growth hormone, correlate directly with the amount of physical contact you receive.

Massage also cues relaxation in your nervous system. One of the biggest benefits of massage is that it feels great, especially if you're in pain. Nerves that carry information about the sensation of touch to the brain are more heavily myelinated than the nerves that carry information about pain, so touch information travels faster than pain information. Therefore, you instinctively rub the skin around a painful area; the touch sensation temporarily drowns out the pain sensation, and you're given a moment of relief.

Massage also feels good because it temporarily reduces muscle tension. Pressing on tight muscles lengthens them in the same way that gentle prolonged static stretching does, and after an hour or so of this manual lengthening you may stand up feeling like your muscles are made of jelly. If your massage therapist applies a great deal of pressure, your stretch reflex may be activated immediately, making you feel tight and sore soon after a massage. A good rule of thumb is that if you feel pain during a massage, you're probably going to feel some soreness afterward as well. While it can be difficult or awkward in the moment, it's better to ask your massage therapist to press more gently than to suffer the consequences. It is not necessary to apply a painful amount of pressure to reap the benefits of a massage. Moreover, if you're in pain, a deep massage can increase and prolong your pain by making your muscles tighter.

Lastly, massage temporarily softens connective tissues, which increases flexibility and range of motion. Tendons, ligaments, fascia (which surrounds, supports, and separates structures of the body), and scar tissue (which forms to heal an injury) are all made of collagen fibers arranged in varying patterns and densities. As muscles become habitually tighter and movement decreases, connective tissues also respond by tightening. Movement and heat can make these collagen structures more flexible and fluid.

For people with chronic pain, the most beneficial aspect of massage may be that it lowers stress, thereby reducing the sensation of pain and reactivity of the nervous system. However, a massage by itself is not enough to change deeply learned habitual movements or your resting level of muscle tension. The sensory awareness that can be gained through massage is valuable, but if it isn't followed by actual motor education in the form of voluntary movement, little lasting progress will be made. You must actively retrain your nervous system, and you can't do that with massage alone.

Brain Balance

First, you must make sure your brain is balanced. Without a balanced nervous system, your efforts to eliminate chronic pain will be wasted. Many things can cause brain imbalances. Most common are head injuries and exposure to electromagnetic radiation from personal wireless devices. Things that increase brain imbalance risk factors include:

- Using Bluetooth devices and cell phones, walkie talkies, using desktop and laptop computers and iPads.

- Eating processed foods that have MSG.

- Consuming drinks containing artificial sweeteners and drinking fluoridated water.

- Leading a stressful life.

- Not getting enough quality sleep.

Brain Balancing Using Affirmations

Studies show that when the thymus gland is balanced, both hemispheres of the brain also remain balanced and serve to lower chronic pain. The nice thing about affirmations is that they don't cost you anything; you just must repeat the affirmations regularly throughout the day to keep your brain in balance. You need to "feel" the words to get full benefits. The following is a list of daily affirmations:

- I have faith, gratitude, trust, love and courage.

- I'm modest, I'm humble and tolerant.

- I'm clean and good, I deserve to be loved.

- I'm content and tranquil.

- I have forgiveness in my heart.

- My life energy is high, life is full of love.

Brain Balancing Music

Brain balancing music encourages a balanced nervous system and balances both hemispheres of the brain. Brain balancing music uses three coordinated methods: "primordial sounds", "brainwave entrainment", and "multi-layered music" to bring the mind-body into a deeply relaxed and balanced state. You must listen to the music daily to maintain your brain balance which is crucial for health and healing of chronic pain.

Avoid GMO foods

GMO or genetically modified organisms have been introduced to our diets over the past decade. As of this writing, the GMO foods are not labeled in the U. S. So, the average American's is unconsciously consuming GMO rich canola oil, sugar. beets, corn, soy and cottonseed oil. GMO foods can cause all sorts of gastrointestinal problems, allergies, weight gain, and immune problems. Avoiding GMO foods can reduce or even eliminate many health problems, including chronic pain.

Emotional Freedom Techniques

This amazing technique deals swiftly with all sorts of emotional pain and has an infinite number of applications. EFT has been around for quite a while and is now used in many hospitals and psych units throughout the world by professional psychologists and psychiatrists who are continuing to get very positive results with severe emotional pain and trauma.

There is no doubt that strong emotions can be very painful things and it is now recognized that emotion follows thought. Therefore, psychiatrists spend years talking about trauma and trying to uncover triggers and thoughts that cause bad feelings, depression, phobias and the like.

EFT is a great way to deal with all fear though you will have to be thorough. Really look at all the different aspects of that fear and treat each one with a very specific opening statement.

Emotional Freedom Technique (EFT) or tapping requires that you tap specific acupressure points on the torso, hands and on the head in order to clear energy blocks caused by negative emotions and feelings.

What you do is tap lightly on each of them. You get used to doing this very quickly, and when you have been using EFT for a while you can just do a few taps here and there, maybe on your collarbone or under your eye, for rapid relief.

Generally tapping involves two stages. In the first stage you are tapping to express the negative emotions. This stage of tapping will last if you have an emotional charge, continual tapping will bring that charge down to a minimal level.

The second stage includes reframing the condition positively where you choose a positive emotion or thought to replace the negative ones. The cool thing is you can't tap incorrectly; your intention is enough to make it work correctly. Even without tapping the right acupressure points, you will still release the negative energy from your body.

Chapter 10   Step by Step Instructions to Strengthen your Vagus Nerve to Upgrade Your Whole Body

The vagal pathway is an arrangement of nerves that interfaces outward from the cerebrum and directs numerous organs in the body – the heart, lungs, gut, liver and more

The current drug regards singular organs as the zone of illness and disregards the way that your mind and sensory system instruct your organs. Your organs normally send a status check to your cerebrum through the vagus nerve to give an account of how things are going.

It's a two-way road. When everything's working out in a good way, your cerebrum keeps up business as usual. At the point when an organ is battling, it can move toward your cerebrum for more assets. At the point when it's the ideal opportunity for your body to spring to activity, your vagus nerve conveys the sign from your cerebrum to your organs to back off.

To ensure nothing is lost in interpretation, your vagus nerve should be in working request. Your mind and organs rely upon your vagal pathways to control things like:

- Yearning hormones and nourishment intake

- Inflammation

- Nervousness and fight-or-flight

- The safe response

Since the vagus nerves are associated with so a lot, it must be working appropriately. Peruse on to discover how you can bolster your vagus nerve using vagal conditioning.

It's cliché, but take deep breaths

There's an association between breath and pulse, which is adjusted by the vagus nerve. That's the reason ordinary yoga practice diminishes by and large stress.

Yoga breathing and guided breathing activities, quiet your pulse and lower your blood pressure. Breathing activities expanded vagal tone and successfully oversaw prehypertension in an exploratory group.

In one examination, slow breathing activities improved autonomic capacities in sound members. Quick breathing didn't. That's since quick breathing makes your body believe you're running from predators. That sets off your body's alerts and initiates a pressure reaction.

Box breathing for s.o.s.

In case you're terrified or going to blow a gasket, attempt box relaxing.

1. Breathe in for a check of four.

2. Hold for a check of four.

3. Breathe out for a check of four.

4. Sit tight for a check of four.

5. Rehash until your hands are back on the controls.

A primary couple of times, follow your finger in a square example noticeable all around. It'll assist you with recollecting how to do it when you're fatigued.

The slow development of your lungs signs to your heart to back off, which sends a sentiment of quiet all through your whole sensory system. Your vagus nerve associates the entirety of this flagging and discharges acetylcholine, a quieting synthetic you can give yourself a fix of whenever by doing unwinding systems.

Relax, LITERALLY

Becoming acclimated to the virus conditions the vagus reaction, which eases back the actuation of the thoughtful sensory system. Customary virus impacts quantifiably lessen pressure markers. Cold presentation calmed indications of sorrow and uneasiness perhaps balanced by the vagus nerve.

Invigorating the vagal pathways animates digestion. When rodents' absorption eased back down because of tension, cold introduction re-enacted the gastric nerves and got everything moving once more. Everything occurred through vagal pathways.

Keep your gut happy

Have you ever known about the gut-cerebrum pivot? That alludes to the microorganisms in your stomach related framework speaking with your mind.

Your microbiome is the biological system of well-disposed microorganisms in your body and on your skin. Regularly, when somebody discusses the microbiome, they're discussing the microorganisms in your digestion tracts and colon.

As the study of the microbiome fabricates, established researchers investigate an ever-increasing number of ways the microbiome influences your whole body. Research on the association between the microbiome and temperament is extending, and correspondence among gut and mind relies on — shock — the vagus nerve.

Concentrates on creature models and people bolster the possibility that a flourishing microbiome controls tension and improves your state of mind. A portion of the exploration analyzed this impact with and without an unblemished vagus nerve, to check whether vagal pathways have anything to do with it.

Rats who enhanced with specific strains of probiotics demonstrated declines in uneasiness and discouragement pointers, however not in creatures whose vagus nerves were cut before the experiment.

Specialists see the useful impacts of probiotics on temperament in humans. Healthy ladies who ate aged nourishments for about a month demonstrated positive changes in mind movement, especially in the pieces of the cerebrum that control feeling and sensation From the creature examines, and from what researchers think about the vagus nerve as of now, you can make a strong conjecture that the gut-mind correspondence here occurs through the vagus nerve.

An ideal approach to help your intestinal vegetation is to get a thorough microbiome test like Viome. Viome is a test-at-home pack that you use to profile your microbiome effectively, and afterward, you get customized dietary proposals to bring you once again into balance.

Discover your safety cues

Vagus nerve master Dr. Stephen Porges built up Polyvagal Theory (more on that on a scene of Bulletproof Radio), which spreads out a choice procedure of sorts that decides if battle or-flight actuates. You are not aware of this procedure — everything occurs out of sight, and various parts of the vagus nerve actuate because of various circumstances.

At the point when you experience an alarming improvement, the principal layer to traverse is the one that reacts to social correspondence — verbal language, non-verbal communication, vocal tone, and other nonverbal cues. If the upgrade is too solid even to consider reasoning through, your mind initiates the battle or flight reaction. At the point when that falls flat, the crudest dread reaction is feigning unconsciousness — feeling solidified.

At the point when you realize your dread is unreasonable, you can utilize wellbeing prompts to stop alarm at the main layer and prevent your cerebrum from finding a workable pace or-flight reaction. Here are a few things you can attempt.

Utilize soothing voices

In his meeting on Bulletproof Radio, Stephen Porges clarifies one way this marvel is designed in kids. Youngsters are quantifiably quieted by prosodic (sing-song) talking, otherwise called "mothers'." Waldorf schools train instructors to embrace this tone to keep up a quiet and cheerful study hall. If you've visited your local play area in the first part of the day, you've seen it in real life.

Modifying your tone of discourse works for grown-ups, as well. Guided reflections, either face to face or recorded, receive a moderate, musical tone of talking. Utilizing the voice as an unwinding signal persuades your cerebrum into a casual state quicker than an ordinary conversational tone would.

Train your safety cues

With a little practice, you can prepare your psyche to have a sense of security. Wellbeing signs prevent your dread and tension reactions from kicking in.

One approach to do this is to make your "sheltered spot" or "upbeat spot" while you're quiet. To do this, you envision you're at a spot where you're calm and feeling content and quiet. Use as a lot of tangible data as you can – envision the sights, smells, sounds, and so forth.

Practice this representation frequently. That way, when you start feeling dreadful or irate, you can start the "protected spot" absent a lot of exertion. It's there when you need it.

Deal with YOUR MYELIN

Your vagus nerve is myelinated, which implies it's canvassed in a defensive covering of fat that protects it and enables the signs to go through effectively. At the point when myelin on any nerve separates, the nerve doesn't fill in too. Peruse this post to become familiar with how to adore your myelin.

Precisely IMPLANTED ELECTRICAL VAGUS NERVE STIMULATOR

The vagus nerve initiates the insusceptible framework when you're battling something. Doctors utilize this information for treatment by invigorating the vagus nerve with power and pharmaceuticals to treat provocative disorders. Doctors precisely embed electric vagus nerve triggers in patients with extreme epilepsy or discouragement since it hoses the aggravation response.

YOU CAN TONE YOUR BABY'S VAGUS NERVE

A few elements play into the infant's vagal tone. Children who are brought into the world untimely or destined to moms who had discouragement and uneasiness during pregnancy have a low vagal tone.

If you were experiencing a few things during pregnancy, don't stress. You can help tone your child's vagal pathways with typical holding practices and cherishing care.

Cold showers ought to likely hold up until junior is mature enough to consent to it. During the infant years, newborn child back rub and kangaroo care (holding infant skin-to-skin) help children's vagal tone develop. If your children are past the infant organize, you can work with them on a portion of the adult approaches to condition the vagus nerve, such as breathing procedures and cold impacts in the shower.

A back rub, a yoga class, and a couple of moments of goosebumps in the shower are presumably justified, despite all the trouble thinking about that the advantages of vagal nerve conditioning stretch out to each significant organ in your body and back. For more approaches to help your entire framework, head-to-toe, pop your data into the crate underneath, so you don't miss a thing.

Is there a role for vagus nerve stimulation in the treatment of posttraumatic stress disorder?

Posttraumatic stress disorder (PTSD) creates in people who have been presented to injury and subsequently languish trouble or practical debilitation over at any multi rate-month. Side effects incorporate sentiments of re-encountering the horrendous mishap, staying away from tokens of the injury, elevated nervousness and excitement, and negative contemplations or emotions. Ongoing cataclysmic events, mass shootings, militant psychological assaults, and urban areas under attack add to the worldwide weight of PTSD which, as indicated by a recent report, influences 4–6% of the worldwide populace, although most of the injuries are identified with mishaps and sexual or physical savagery. Shockingly, there is no known fix, and flow medicines are not compelling for all patients. A PTSD psychopharmacology working gathering as of late distributed their accord articulation calling for a quick activity to address the emergency in PTSD treatment, referring to three significant concerns. In the first place, just two medications (sertraline and paroxetine) are affirmed by the US FDA for the treatment of PTSD. These prescriptions diminish manifestation seriousness; however, they may not deliver total abatement of side effects. The subsequent concern is identified with polypharmacy. PTSD patients are recommended meds to address every one of their numerous one of a kind and various indications including tension, trouble resting, sexual brokenness, despondency, and constant torment, with inadequate experimental examinations of medication collaborations. The high comorbidity among PTSD and dependence gives further difficulties to pharmacotherapies. The third significant concern is the absence of progressions in the treatment of PTSD; no new drugs have been endorsed since 2001.

Going past indication alleviation, the 'highest quality level' injury centered way to deal with treating PTSD pathology is presentation-based treatment, where patients are presented to the tokens of the injury until they figure out how to connect these signs with security. Although there is acceptable proof for adequacy with this methodology, not all patients completely react to the treatment. Exposure treatment relies upon the way toward stifling the adapted dread memory, which is overwhelmed by another memory that creates through rehashed exposures. The patients with uneasiness issues and PTSD show disabilities in their capacity to smother molded feelings of fear, which could add to the advancement of clutters and may meddle with progress in treatment. Since the memory of the injury isn't lost in any case, rather, enhancements through treatment rely upon newly learned affiliations that horrible rival affiliations, the parity of the two recollections can move after some time, prompting backslide. Different difficulties remember the trouble for perceiving and dousing apprehension of every single molded improvement, and a high dropout rate, which isn't astounding given that evasion is one of the side effects of PTSD.

Numerous creatures investigate labs have put forth attempts to create adjunctive medicines to quicken or upgrade the impacts of presentation-based treatments. Spearheading work did by Michael Davis indicated that organization of the psychological improving medication d-cycloserine before presenting rodents to unreinforced adapted signs upgraded annihilation, and he and his associates along these lines deciphered the disclosure when they found that d-cycloserine additionally upgraded the impacts of presentation treatment in patients with explicit fears. Notwithstanding, aftereffects of studies surveying the impacts of psychological enhancers as subordinates to presentation treatment are blended on account of PTSD. A potential clarification is that medications given before introduction treatment sessions risk fortifying negative affiliations if presentation produces uneasiness. Anxiolytic medications have been attempted because of proof that these medications ought to improve decency and lessen the nervousness reaction during the introduction. In any case, results show that anxiolytic medications don't upgrade the impacts of introduction treatment. One clarification is that the uneasiness reaction is required for accomplishment in presentation treatment since patients must learn not to fear their fear reaction.

On the other hand, similarly, as stress can upgrade the capacity of horrendous accidents, the nervousness reaction may improve the solidification of the eradication memory. Predictable with this, anxiolytic medications will, in general, hinder memory union. A perfect extra would take advantage of the systems that upgrade the solidification of horrible recollections to advance eradication recollections that are similarly as solid, at the same time bypassing or staying away from the aversive pressure reaction.

Developing proof proposes that vagus nerve stimulation (VNS) might be an advantageous extra to introduction-based treatments through its explicit blending improvement of memory union and neural pliancy. Enthusiasm for the vagus nerve (the tenth cranial nerve) as a neuromodulator originates from a very long while of research showing that the vagus nerve fills in as a scaffold between the fringe autonomic sensory system and the cerebrum. It flags the cerebrum during times of elevated thoughtful action, advancing quick stockpiling of recollections that are significant for endurance. As a component of the parasympathetic nervous system, the actuation of the vagus nerve neutralizes the thoughtful pressure reaction.

VNS improves memory in rats and people, proposing that blending VNS with the unreinforced presentation to adapted signals may upgrade the solidification of the termination memory. Reliable with this speculation, we found that VNS upgraded the elimination of molded fear in rats. Broad proof demonstrates that VNS advances neural pliancy, particularly when it is combined with preparing, and this impact includes VNS tweak of the locus coeruleus noradrenergic framework. We have watched versatility impacts in the eradication related infralimbic prefrontal cortex – basolateral amygdala pathway in the wake of matching VNS with an introduction to unreinforced adapted signs, proposing that VNS-upgraded annihilation might be vigorous, dependable, and less helpless to backslide. In an ongoing report, we found that VNS additionally improved the eradication of adapted dread in a rodent model of PTSD. These rodents express a considerable lot of the biomarkers and social phenotypes that are related to PTSD and, critically, they are impervious to termination of adapted fear. We found that the VNS organization during elimination sessions turned around this eradication disability and forestalled the arrival of dread. VNS-treated rodents likewise performed better on trial of tension, excitement, shirking, and social cooperation's multi-week later, showing that inversion of the term disability meant enhancements in other PTSD manifestations.

Furthermore, interminable, unpaired VNS, as is utilized in the treatment of epilepsy and misery, improved execution on the Hamilton Anxiety Scale in certain patients with uneasiness issue, and decreased nervousness like conduct in rats. The impacts of VNS on annihilation in our examinations are not seen when the VNS is controlled 30 min to 1 h in the wake of preparing. Subsequently, VNS alone isn't adequate to diminish the dread reaction. These discoveries propose that VNS may diminish nervousness, however matching explicit versatility and memory adjustment is essential for eradication upgrade. Our ongoing, unpublished discoveries demonstrate that rodents are bound to investigate the open arms of a raised in addition to labyrinth following accepting VNS, recommending that VNS produces an intense anxiolytic impact. Moreover, corticosterone levels expanded altogether in hoax treated rodents following testing on the raised in addition to labyrinth, yet such an expansion was not seen in VNS-treated rodents. This work ought to be reproduced in different settings, however it is an empowering initial move toward recognizing an aide treatment that may improve pass ableness and viability in presentation-based treatments.

Conclusion

Your diet is going to facilitate just about everything in your body. If your body does not have the nutrients that it needs, it will not be able to function properly, and you will find that you do not properly manage to produce the right stimulation and tone that you need. You must ensure that your vagus nerve has the support that it needs to support your entire body if you want to be able to rely on it, and that will primarily come from diet.

You will find that omega-3 fatty acids will be a great addition to your diet. This is not only healthy for your brain; it is good for your nerves as well. It will help you facilitate all sorts of healthy neuronal connections that will then allow the vagus nerve to work the way that it is supposed to. You may try to add fatty fish to your diet to help meet this need, for example—you may choose to eat salmon or tuna. However, be mindful of the fact that seafood can oftentimes come along with mercury, so try to eat fish with lower mercury content whenever you can.

Beyond that, you will want to eat a wide range of foods as often as you can. You will want to ensure that you are eating healthy fruits and vegetables to aid in digestion and support your body properly. When you eat plenty of fruits and vegetables, especially fibrous ones, you will be directly supporting your gut bacteria, giving them the proper nutrition that they need to function. Beyond just that, everyone should be eating a rainbow every day—try to make sure that the foods that you eat cover the entire spectrum of colors for optimal digestion and health.

Along those same lines, you want to make sure that you support the vagus nerve by ensuring that you have healthy gut bacteria present. Remember, the vagus nerve primarily deals with this area of the body—it is responsible for making sure that you are getting the food you need, and your gut bacteria will alter it. The bacteria in your digestive tract plays more of a role than just digesting your food—it also creates neurotransmitters, and it has been found that anxiety and depression can be related back to having a poor balance of gut bacteria in the first place. If you realize that your gut bacteria are out of sorts, you probably are currently suffering from either digestive issues or you have noticed that your mood is not what it used to be. No matter the reason or why you feel the way that you do, it is important for you to stop and think that maybe you should try treating the gut with probiotics.

You will want to find probiotics that are rich in both lactobacillus Rhamnosus and Bifidobacterium Longum. These two bacteria strains have been found to improve vagus nerve function while also reducing stress hormone production within animals. By making sure that you are taking a probiotic on a regular basis, you will likely see an improvement in your mood.

Exercise is another crucial step in ensuring that your vagus nerve stays healthy. Your vagus nerve is connected to just about every part of your vital organs. It is innervating your heart and lungs, which both get a workout when you are exercising yourself. This means that you are naturally training your vagus nerve at the same time. When you use your vagus nerve on the regular, you will find that you are beginning to see those changes in behaviors that you need. When you exercise, you will tone your heart, your breathing, and even your vagus nerve.

When you want to exercise your vagus nerve, you will be wanting to look for exercises that will either stretch the chest and abdominal muscles to directly strengthen the vagus nerve through direct stimulation, or you will want to use cardio exercise to get the heart pumping and the blood moving. When you do so on the regular, your vagus nerve will have to engage regularly. You can see that the vagus nerve activates more as well with how the time that it takes your body to recover from this stress quickly begins to dwindle. Because it will get so used to activating on the regular, you will find that it is commonly growing stronger and more active in general, which is good news for you. The stronger your vagus nerve, the better your emotional regulation and health will become.

Finally, we are going to look at social relationships and your vagus nerve. When you are socializing with someone else, your vagus nerve is already active. It is activating the social engagement system—the part of your brain that is entirely interested in interacting more with those around you. When you activate this part of your brain, you usually find that you are calmer in general. You will literally be triggering the activity of the "tend and befriend" mode of your brain. This is important—when you look at this part of the brain, you begin to realize something: You are using your vagus nerve.

This makes sense. When you consider that the vagus nerve passes through the face, and the vagus nerve facilitates emotional regulation, you would think that it would be strongly related to how likely or how little you want to socialize with other people. When you activate this system within the brain, you are happier to work with other people. You are open to communication and more likely to be smiling and happy in general.

What is interesting, however, is the fact that many social activities also activate the vagus nerve as well. A good, long laugh with someone else is going to be triggering the vagus nerve as well. It does this through a few different methods. Firstly, you must consider that laughing is loud. When you laugh with someone else, you are likely to laugh deeper and louder. Laughing also forces you to take big, deep breaths, which will also engage the vagus nerve. Beyond that, however, you will also see that you are smiling. Smiling is yet another way that you can trigger your vagus nerve to activate as well, thanks to the fact that it innervates all those muscles.

Essentially, just being social with other people is enough for you to stimulate the vagus nerve and kick it into action. When you do this, you will find that you are much more likely to facilitate it growing healthier and stronger.

As you can see, there are several different life choices that you can make that will sort of support the development of the vagus nerve. When you have a healthy social life, you are much more likely to laugh regularly. You are much more likely to smile and facilitate a good, strong social engagement response. When you eat well and use probiotics, you ensure that you have the proper microbiota to deal with what your body needs to do as well as to make sure that you are getting all sorts of good neurotransmitters produced within your body. When you stop and make sure that you are exercising, you directly train your vagus nerve as well.

Beyond just training the vagus nerve, however, you may notice that all four of those choices that you can make will also facilitate a healthier lifestyle in general. You will be healthier physically and mentally, not only because of the vagus nerve but also because you have made the healthy choices that your body needed.